Email Me A Copy!

Email Me A Copy!

A compilation of some of the
best messages ever sent through the
workplace (2006-2008)

Compiled by
Robert D. Kramer

ISBN 13: 978-0-9895028-3-2

Published in the United States of America

Table of Contents

Introduction

As a background, I am a United States Air Force Vet and I have spent over 40-years employed in corporate America. Early on in my career, people would come up to me and give me a piece of paper with some sort of joke, story, or just an item of interest to read. Usually I got a laugh from it or a comment such as: "That's Kool," and "Make me a copy of that." Then after the onrush of the computers in our business atmosphere, I would get emails from friends and acquaintances of these same types of jokes, stories or items of interest. I would usually laugh, and I almost always printed a copy. Some were dirty in nature, some political, some serious, some short and some had some length to them—you get the picture. I'm sure you have received them too.

I kept most all those copies over the years, and in this book I want to share them with you. I obviously transcribed them onto my computer for the book, but I wrote them just as they were received; spelling, punctuation, language, etc. I think if I put all the copies in a pile, it would probably be 12" to 15" high.

As you read this book, you may see a passage that is duplicated. That means different people sent me that communication in different years. Kind of like, it "keeps on giving."

I suspect, as you read these jokes/passages from our past, you will probably say to yourself, "I remember that!" And with others, you might say, "That was Kool," or "I can relate to that." Either way, I hope you enjoy the book as much as I have enjoyed receiving these jokes, stories and passages over the years.

I'm sure as you read these jokes/passages from our past, you may say to yourself, "I remember that." And with others, you might say,

"That was cool," or "I can relate to that." Either way, I hope you enjoy the book as much as I have enjoyed receiving these jokes, stories and passages over the years.

2006

PICK UP LINE

Having already downed a few power drinks, she turned around, faced him, looked him straight in the eye and said, "Listen up, Buddy, I screw anybody, anytime, anywhere, your place, my place, in the car, front door, back door, on the ground, standing up, sitting down, naked or with clothes on, dirty, clean…. It doesn't matter to me. I've been doing it ever since I got out of college and I just love it."

Eyes now wide with interest, he responded, "No kidding. I'm a lawyer, too. What firm are you with?"

TO ALL NEW JERSEYANS

If you ever lived in Jersey…you'll appreciate this. With its few problems, it's still one of the best places in the world to live!! You don't have to worry about being blown away, washed away, or cooked to death!!

- New Jersey is a peninsula. Highlands, New Jersey has the highest elevation along the entire eastern seaboard, from Maine to Florida.

- New Jersey is the only state where all of its counties are classified as metropolitan areas.

- New Jersey has more race horses than Kentucky.

- New Jersey has more Cubans in Union City (1 sq. mil) than Havana, Cuba.

- New Jersey has the densest system of highways and railroads in the US.

- New Jersey has the highest cost of living.

- New Jersey has the highest cost of auto insurance.

- New Jersey has the highest property taxes in the nation.

- New Jersey has the most diners in the world and is sometimes referred to as the "Diner Capital of the World."

- New Jersey is home to the original Mystery Pork Parts Club, (no, not Spam): Taylor Ham and Port Roll.

- Home to the less mysterious but the best Italian hot dogs and Italian sausage w/peppers and onions.

- North New Jersey is home to the Statute of Liberty and Ellis Island.

- The Passaic River was the site of the first submarine ride by inventor John P. Holland.

- New Jersey has 50+ resort cities and towns; some of the nation's most famous: Asbury Park, Wildwood, Atlantic City, Seaside Heights, Long Branch, and Cape May.

- New Jersey is a leading technology & industrial state and is the largest chemical producing state in the nation when you include pharmaceuticals.

- Jersey tomatoes are known the world over as being the best you can buy.

- New Jersey is the world leader in blueberry and cranberry production.

- Here's to New Jersey – the toast of the country! In 1642, the first brewery in America opened in Hoboken.

- New Jersey rocks! The famous Les Paul invented the first solid body electric guitar in Mahwah, in 1940.

- New Jersey is a major seaport state with the largest seaport in the US, located in Elizabeth. Nearly 80% of what our nation imports comes through Elizabeth Seaport first.

- New Jersey is home to one of the nation's busiest airports – Liberty International (Newark).

- George Washington slept there.

- Several important Revolutionary War battles were fought on New Jersey soil, led by General George Washington.

- The light bulb, phonograph (record player), and motion picture projector, were invented by Thomas Edison in his Menlo Park, NJ, laboratory.

- New Jersey boasts the first town ever lit by incandescent bulbs.

- The first seaplane was built in Keyport, NJ.

- The first airmail (to Chicago) was started from Keyport, NJ.

- The first phonograph records were made in Camden, NJ.

- New Jersey was home to the Miss America Pageant held in Atlantic City.

- The game Monopoly, played all over the world, named the streets on its playing board after the actual streets in Atlantic City.

- And, Atlantic City has the longest boardwalk in the world, not to mention the best salt water taffy.

- New Jersey has the largest petroleum containment area outside of the Middle East countries.

- The first Indian Reservation was in New Jersey, in the Wachung Mountains.

- New Jersey has the tallest water-tower in the world, (Union, NJ).

- New Jersey had the first medical center, in Jersey City.

- The Pulaski SkyWay, from Jersey City to Newark, was the first skyway highway.

- New Jersey built the first tunnel under a river, the Hudson (Holland Tunnel).

- The first baseball game was played in Hoboken, which is also the birthplace of Frank Sinatra.

- The first intercollegiate football game was played in New Brunswick in 1889 (Rutgers and Princeton).

- The first drive-in movie theater was opened in Camden (but they're all gone now!).

- New Jersey is home to both of "New York's" pro football teams!

- The first radio station and broadcast was in Paterson.

- The first FM radio broadcast was made from Alpine by Maj. Thomas Armstrong.

- The Great Falls in Paterson, on the Passaic River is the 2nd largest waterfall on the East Coast of the US.

- You know you're from Jersey when:

  - You don't think of fruit when people mention "The Oranges."
  - You know that it's called Great Adventure, not Six Flags.
  - A good, quick breakfast is a hard roll with butter.
  - You've known the way to Seaside Heights since you were seven.
  - You've eaten at a diner, when you were drunk, at 3 A.M.
  - You know that the state isn't one big oil refinery.
  - At least three people in your family still love Bruce Springsteen, and you know the town Jon Bon Jovi is from.
  - You know what a 'jug handle" is.
  - You know that WaWa is a convenience store.
  - You know that the state isn't all farmland.
  - You know that there are no "beaches" in New Jersey – there's the shore – and you don't go "to the shore," you go

"down the shore." And when you are there, you're not "at the shore," you are "down the shore."

- You know how to properly negotiate a circle.
- You knew that the last sentence had to do with driving.
- You know that this is the only "New" state that doesn't require "New" to identify it (try Mexico, York, Hampshire – doesn't work, does it).
- You know that a "White Castle" is the name of BOTH a fast food chain and a fast food sandwich.
- You consider putting mayo on a corned beef sandwich a sacrilege.
- You don't think "What exit?" is very funny.
- You know that people from the 609 area code are "a little different." Yes, they are.
- You know that no respectable New Jerseyian goes to Princeton – that's for out-of-stater's.
- The Jets-Giants game has started fights at your school or local bars.
- You live within 20 minutes of at least three different malls.
- You refer to all highways and interstates by their numbers.
- Every year you have at least one kid in your class named Tony.
- You know the location of every clip shown in the Sopranos opening credits.
- You've gotten on the wrong highway trying to get out of the mall.
- You know that people from North Jersey go to Seaside Heights, people from Central Jersey go to Belmar, and

people from South Jersey go to Wildwood – It can be no other way.

- You weren't raised in New Jersey – you were raised in either North Jersey, Central Jersey or South Jersey.

- You don't consider Newark or Camden to actually be part of the state.

- You remember the stores Korvette's, Two Guys, Rickel's, Channel, Bamberger's and Orbach's.

- You remember Palisades Amusement Park.

- You've had a boardwalk cheese steak and vinegar fries.

- You start planning for Memorial Day weekend in February.

And finally…

- You've NEVER, NEVER, NEVER, EVER pumped your own gas!

SOUTHERNERS CAN BE SO POLITE

Atlanta ARC: Tower to Saudi Air 511 – You are cleared to land eastbound on runway 9R.

Saudi Air: Thank you Atlanta ATC, Acknowledge cleared to land on infidel's runway 9R - Allah be Praised.

Atlanta ATC: Tower to Iran Air 711 – You are cleared to land westbound on runway 9R.

Iran Air: Thank you Atlanta ATC. We are cleared to land on infidel's runway 9R. Allah is Great.

Pause…

Saudi Air: Atlanta ATC – Atlanta ATC.

Atlanta ATC: Go ahead Saudi Air 511.

Saudi Air: You have cleared both our aircrafts for the same runway going in opposite directions. We are on a collision course. Instructions, please.

Atlanta ATC: Well bless your hearts. And praise Jesus. Y'all be careful now and tell Allah 'hey' for us.

SPRING CLASSES FOR MEN AT THE ADULT LEARNING CENTER

NOTE: Due to the complexity and difficulty level of their contents, class sizes will be limited to 8 participants maximum.

Class 1
How To Fill Up The Ice Cube trays – Step by Step, with Slide Presentation
Meets 4 weeks, Monday and Wednesday for 2 hours beginning at 7:00 PM

Class 2
The Toilet Paper Roll – Does It Change Itself? Round Table Discussion.
Meets 2 weeks, Saturday 12:00 for 2 hours.

Class 3
Is It Possible To Urinate Using The Technique Of Lifting The Seat and Avoiding The Floor, Walls and Nearby Bathtub?
Meets 4 weeks, Saturday 10:00 PM for 2 hours.

Class 4
Fundamental Differences Between The Laundry Hamper and The Floor - -Pictures and Explanatory Graphics.
Meets Saturdays at 2:00 PM for 3 weeks.

Class 5
Dinner Dishes -- Can They Levitate and Fly Into the Kitchen Sink? Examples on Video.
Meets 4 weeks, Tuesday and Thursday for 2 hours beginning at 7:00 PM

Class 6

Loss Of Identity – Losing The Remote To Your Significant Other. Help Line Support and Support Groups.

Meets 4 weeks, Friday and Sunday 7:00 PM

Class 7

Learning How To Find Things - - Starting With Looking In The Right Places And Not Turning The House Upside Down While Screaming. Open Form.

Monday at 8:00 PM 2 hours.

Class 8

Health Watch - - Bringing Her Flowers Is Not Harmful To Your Health. Graphics and Audio Tapes.

Three nights; Monday, Wednesday, Friday at 7:00 PM for 2 hours.

Class 9

Real Men Ask For Directions When Lost – Real Life Testimonials.

Tuesdays at 6:00 PM Location to be determined.

Class 10

Is It Generally Impossible To Sit Quietly While She Parallel Parks? Driving Simulations.

4 weeks, Saturday's noon, 2 hours.

Class 11

Learning to Live - - Basic Differences Between Mother and Wife. Online Classes and Role-playing.

Tuesdays at 7:00 PM, location to be determined.

Class 12

How To Be the Ideal Shopping Companion. Relaxation Exercises, Meditation and Breathing Techniques.

Meets 4 weeks, Tuesday and Thursday for 2 hours beginning at 7:00 PM

Class 13
How to Fight Cerebral Atrophy - - Remembering Birthdays, Anniversaries and Other Important Dates and Calling When You're Going To Be Late.
Cerebral Shock Therapy Sessions and Full Lobotomies Offered.
Three nights; Monday, Wednesday, Friday at 7:00 PM 2 hours.

Class 14
The Stove/Oven - - What It Is and How It Is Used. Live Demonstrations.
Tuesdays at 6:00 PM, location to be determined.

Upon completion of any of the above courses, diplomas will be issued to the survivors.

WEST VIRGINIA BLONDE

Two bored casino dealers are waiting at the craps table. A very attractive blonde woman from West Virginia arrives and bets $20,000 on a single roll of the dice.

She said, "I hoped y'all don't mind, but I feel much luckier when I'm completely nude." With that, she stripped down, rolled the dice and yelled, "Come on, baby, Mama needs new clothes!"

As the dice came to a stop, she jumped up and down and squealed…"Yes! Yes! I WON! I WON!" She hugged each of the dealers, and then picked up her winnings and her clothes and quickly departed. The dealers stared at each other dumbfounded. Finally, one of them asked, "What did she roll?"

The other answered, "I don't know – I thought you were watching."

Moral: Not all West Virginians are stupid and not all blonds are dumb, but all men are men.

THINGS TO KNOW

1. Budweiser beer conditions the hair.
2. Pam cooking spray will dry finger nail polish.
3. Cool Whip will condition you hair in 15 minutes.
4. Mayonnaise will KILL LICE, it will also condition your hair.
5. Elmer's Glue – paint on your face, allow it to dry, peel off and see the dead skin and blackheads.
6. Shiny Hair – use brewed Lipton Tea.
7. Sunburn – empty a large jar of Nestea into your bath water.
8. Minor burn – Colgate or Crest toothpaste.
9. Burn your tongue? Put some sugar on it!
10. Arthritis? WD-40 spray and rub in, kill insect stings too.
11. See Stings – meat tenderizer.
12. Chigger bite – Preparation H.
13. Puffy eyes – Preparation H.
14. Paper cut – crazy glue or chap stick (glue is used instead of sutures at most hospitals).
15. Stinky feet – Jell-o.
16. Athlete's feet – corn starch.
17. Fungus on toenails or fingernails – Vicks vapor rub.
18. Kool Aid: To clean dishwater pipes. Just put in the detergent section and run a cycle. It will also clean a toilet. (Wow, and we drink this stuff).
19. Kool Aid can be used as a dye in paint, also Kool Aid in Dannon Plain yogurt as a finger paint. Your kids will love it and it won't hurt them if they eat it!

20. Peanut butter – will get scratches out of CD's! Wipe off with a coffee filter paper.

21. Sticking bicycle chain – Pam no-stick cooking spray.

22. Pam: Will also remove paint and grease from your hands. Keep a can in your garage.

23. Peanut butter will remove ink from the face of dolls.

24. When the doll clothes are hard to put on, sprinkle with corn starch and watch them slide on.

25. Heavy dandruff – pour on the vinegar!

26. Body paint – Crisco Mixed with food coloring. Heat the Crisco in the microwave, pour in to an empty film container and mix with the food color of your choice.

27. Tie Dye T-shirt – mix a solution of Kool Aid in a container, tie a rubber band around a section of the T-shirt and soak.

28. Preserving a newspaper clipping – large bottle of club soda and cup of milk of magnesia/ soak for 20 minutes and let dry. It will last for many years!

29. A slinky will hold toast and CD's.

30. To keep goggles and glasses from fogging, coat with Colgate toothpaste.

31. Wine stains, pour on the Morton salt and watch it absorb into the salt.

32. To remove wax – take a paper towel and iron it over the wax stain, it will absorb into the towel.

33. Remove labels of glassware etc. – rub with Peanut butter!

34. Baked on food – fill container with water, get a Bounce paper softener and the static from the Bounce Towel will cause the baked on food to adhere to it. Soaking overnight. Also; you can use 2 Efferdent tablets, soak overnight.

35. Crayon on the wall – Colgate toothpaste and brush it!

36. Dirty grout – Listerine.

37. Stains on clothes – Colgate.

38. Grass stains – Karo Syrup.

39. Grease stains – Coca Cola, it will also remove grease stains from the driveway overnight. We know it will take corrosion from car batteries!

40. Fleas in your carpet? 20 Mule Team Borax – Sprinkle and let stand for 24 hours. Maybe this will work if you get them back again.

41. To keep FRESH FLOWERS longer, add a little Clorox, or 2 Bayer aspirin, or just use 7-Up instead of water.

42. When you go to buy bread in the grocery store, have you ever wondered which is the freshest, so you squeeze for freshness or softness? Did you know that bread is delivered fresh to the store five days a week? Monday, Tuesday, Thursday, Friday and Saturday. Each day has a different color twist tie. They are: Monday – blue, Tuesday – green, Thursday – red, Friday – white, and Saturday – yellow. So if today was Thursday, you would want red twist tie, not white which is Friday's. The colors go alphabetically by color, blue-green-red-white-yellow.

STAY!

I pulled into the crowded parking lot at the Super Wal-Mart Shopping Center and rolled down the car windows to make sure my Labrador Retriever puppy had fresh air.

She was stretched full-out on the back seat and I wanted to impress upon her that she must remain there. I walked to the curb backward, pointing my finger at the car and saying emphatically, "Now you stay. Do you hear me?"

"Stay! Stay!"

The driver of a nearby car, a pretty blonde young lady, gave me a strange look and said, "Why don't you just put it in park?"

STRESS MANAGEMENT

A lecturer, when explaining stress management to an audience, raised a glass of water and asked, "How heavy is this glass of water?"

Answers called out ranged from 20g to 500g.

The lecturer replied, "The absolute weight doesn't matter. It depends on how long you try to hold it. If I hold it for a minute, that's not a problem. If I hold it for an hour, I'll have an ache in my right arm. If I hold it for a day, you'll have to call an ambulance.

In each case, it's the same weight, but the longer I hold it, the heavier it becomes."

He continued, "and that's the way it is with stress management. If we carry our burdens all the time, sooner of later, as the burden becomes increasingly heavy, we won't be able to carry on."

"As with the glass of water, you have to put it down for a while and rest before holding it again. When we're refreshed, we can carry on with the burden."

"So, before you return home tonight, put the burden of work down. Don't carry it home. You can pick it up tomorrow.

"Whatever burdens you're carrying now, let them down for a moment if you can." So, my friend, why not take a while to just simply RELAX.

Put down anything that may be a burden to you right now. Don't pick it up again until after you've rested a while.

Life is short. Enjoy it! Here are some great ways of dealing with the burdens of life:

- Accept that some days you're the pigeon, and some days you're the statue.

- Always keep your words soft and sweet, just in case you have to eat them.

- Always read stuff that will make you look good if you die in the middle of it.

- Drive carefully. It's not only cars that can be recalled by their maker.

- If you can't be kind, as least have the decency to be vague.

- If you lend someone $20 and never see that person again, it was probably worth it.

- It may be that your sole purpose in life is simply to serve as a warning to others.

- Never buy a car you can't push.

- Never put both feet in your mouth at the same time, because! then you won't have a leg to stand on.

- Nobody cares if you can't dance will. Just get up and dance.

- Since it's the early worm that gets eaten by the bird, sleep late.

- When everything's coming your way, you're in the wrong lane.

- Birthdays are good for you. The more you have, the longer you live.

- You may be only one person in the world, but you may also be the world to one person.

- Some mistakes are too much fun to only make once.

- We could learn a lot from crayons…Some are sharp, some are pretty and some are dull. Some have weird names, and all are different colors, but they all have to live in the same box.

- A truly happy person is one who can enjoy the scenery on a detour.

- Have an awesome day and know that someone has thought about you today…. I did.

THE BLONDE DID IT AGAIN

Three women go down to Mexico one night to celebrate college graduation, get drunk, and wake up in jail, only to find that they are to be executed in the morning, though none of them can remember what they did the night before.

The first one, a redhead, is strapped in the electric chair, and is asked if she has any last words. She says, I just graduated from Brigham Young University and believe in the almighty power of God to intervene on the behalf of the innocent.

They throw the switch and nothing happens. They all immediately fall to the floor on their knees; beg for her forgiveness, and release her.

The second one, a brunette, is strapped in and gives her last words, "I just graduated from the Harvard School of Law and I believe in the power of justice to intervene on the part of the innocent."

They throw the switch and, again, nothing happens. Again, they all immediately fall to their knees; beg for her forgiveness, and release her.

The last one, a blonde, is strapped in and says, "Well, I'm from the University of Kentucky and just graduated with a degree in Electrical Engineering, and I'll tell ya right now, y'all ain't gonna electrocute nobody if you don't plug this thing in.

ANOTHER GOODY FOR THE OLD-TIMERS

Mom used to cut chicken, chop eggs and spread mayo on the same cutting board with the same knife and no bleach, but we didn't seem to get food poisoning.

Mom used to defrost hamburger on the counter and I used to eat it raw sometimes, too. Our school sandwiches were wrapped in wax paper in a brown bag, and not in ice pack coolers, but I can't remember getting E. coli.

Almost all of us would have rather gone swimming in the lake instead of the pristine pool (talk about boring), no beach closures then.

The term cell phone would have conjured up a phone in a jail cell, and a pager was the school PA system.

We all took gym, not PE…and risked permanent injury with a pair of high top Ked's (only worn in gym) instead of having cross-training athletic shoes with air cushion soles and built in light reflectors. I can't recall any injuries but they must have happened because they tell us how much safer we are now….

Flunking gym was not an option…even for stupid kids. I guess PE must be much harder than gym.

Speaking of school, we all said prayers, sang the national anthem, and stayed in detention, before schools caught all sorts of negative attention.

We must have had horribly damaged psyches. What an archaic health system we had then. Remember school nurses? Ours wore a hat and everything.

I thought that I was supposed to accomplish something before I was allowed to be proud of myself.

I just can't recall how bored we were without computers, Play Stations, Nintendo, X-box or 270 digital TV cable stations.

Oh yeah…and where was the Benadryl and sterilization kit when I got that bee sting? I could have been killed!

We played 'king of the hill' on piles of gravel left on vacant construction sites, and when we got hurt, Mom pulled out the 48-cent bottle of Mercurochrome (kids liked it better because it didn't sting like iodine did) and then we got our butt spanked. Now it's a trip to the emergency room, followed by a 10-day dose of a $49 bottle of antibiotics, and then Mom calls the attorney to sue the contractor for leaving a horribly vicious pile of gravel where it was such a threat.

We didn't act up at the neighbor's house either, because if we did, we got out butt spanked there and then we got butt spanked again when we got home.

I recall Donny Reynolds from next door coming over and doing his tricks on the front stoop, just before he fell off. Little did his Mom know that she could have owned our house. Instead, she picked him up and swatted him for being such a goof. It was a neighborhood run amuck.

To top it off, not a single person I knew had ever been told that they were from a dysfunctional family. How could we possibly have known that? We needed to get into group therapy and anger management classes. We were obviously so duped by so many societal ills, that we didn't even notice that the entire country wasn't taking Prozac! How did we ever survive?

WORDS WITH TWO MEANINGS

1. THINGY (thing-ee) noun
    Female: Any part under a car's hood.
    Male: The strap fastener on a woman's bra.

2. VULNERABLE (vul-ne-ra-bel) Adverb
    Female: Fully opening up one's self emotionally to another.
    Male: Playing football without a cup.

3. COMMUNICATION (ko-myoo-ni-kay-shon) noun
    Female: The open sharing of thoughts and feelings with one's partner.
    Male: Leaving a note before taking off on a fishing trip with the boys.

4. COMMITMENT (ko-mit-ment) noun
    Female: A desire to get married and raise a family.
    Male: Trying not to hit on other women while out with this one.

5. ENTERTAINMENT (en-ter-tayn-ment) noun
    Female: A good movie, concert, play or book.
    Male: Anything that can be done while drinking beer.

6. FLATULENCE (flach-u-lens) noun
    Female: An embarrassing byproduct of omdogestopm.
    Male: A source of entertainment, self-expression, male bonding.

7. MAKING LOVE (may-king luv) noun

Female: The greatest expression of intimacy a couple can achieve.

Male: Call it whatever you want, just as long as we do it.

8. REMOTE CONTROL (ri-moht kon-trohl) noun
Female: A device for changing from one TV channel to another.

Male: A device for scanning through all 375 channels every 5 minutes.

He Said; She Said

He said...I don't know why you wear a bra; you've got nothing to put in it.
She said...You wear pants don't you?

He said...Shall we try swapping positions tonight?
She said...That's a good idea – you stand by the ironing board while I sit on the sofa...and fart!

He said...What have you been doing with all the grocery money I gave you?
She said...Turn sideways and look in the mirror!

He said...How many men does it take to change a roll of toilet paper?
She said...We don't know; it has never happened.

He said...Why is it difficult to find men who are sensitive, caring and good looking?
She said...They already have boyfriends.

She said...What do you call a woman who knows where her husband is every night?
He said...A widow.

He said...Why are married women heavier than single women?
She said...Single women come home, see what's in the fridge and go to bed. Married women come home, see what's in bed and go to the fridge.

A REVERENTLY THING

A church sign along the side of the road: Staying in bed shouting, "Oh God!" does not constitute going to church.

While driving in Pennsylvania, a family caught up to an Amish carriage. The owner of the carriage obviously had a sense of humor, because attached to the back of the carriage was a hand painted sign, "Energy-efficient vehicle: Runs on oats and grass. Caution: Do not step in exhaust."

A minister waited in line to have his car filled with gas just before a long holiday weekend. The attendant worked quickly, but there where many cars ahead of him in front of the service station. Finally, the attendant motioned him toward a vacant pump. "Reverend," said the young man, "sorry about the delay. It seems as if everyone waits until the last minute to get ready for a long trip." The minister chuckled, "I know what you mean. It's the same in my business."

People want the front of the bus, the back of the church, and the center of attention.

A father was approached by his small son who told him proudly, "I know what the Bible means!" His father smiled and replied, "What do you mean, you 'know' what the Bible means?" The son replied, "I do know!" "Okay, said his father. "So, son, what does the Bible mean?" "That's easy, Daddy. It stands for 'Basic Instructions before Leaving Earth."

Sunday after church, a Mom asked her very young daughter what the lesson was about. The daughter answered, "Don't be scared, you'll get your quilt." Needless to say, the Mom was perplexed. Later in the day, the pastor stopped by for a cup of tea and the Mom asked him what that's morning's Sunday school lesson was about. He said, "Be not afraid, thy comforter is coming."

WELCOME HOME

I sat in my seat of the Boeing 767 waiting for everyone to hurry and stow their carry-ons and grab a seat so we could start what I was sure to be a long, uneventful flight home.

With the huge capacity and slow moving people taking their time to stuff luggage far too big for the overhead and never paying much attention to holding up a growing line behind them, I simply shook my head knowing that this flight was not starting out very well. I was anxious to get home to see my loved ones, so I was focused on my issues and just felt like standing up and yelling for some of these clowns to get their act together.

I knew I couldn't say a word so I just thumbed thru the "Sky Mall" magazine from the seat pocket in front of me. You know it's really getting rough when you resort to the over-priced, useless sky mall crap to break the monotony. With everyone finally seated, we just sat there with the cabin door open and no one in any hurry to get us going although we were well past the scheduled lake off time. No wonder the airline industry is in trouble I told myself.

Just then, the attendant came on the intercom to inform us all that we were being delayed. The entire plane let out a collective groan.

She resumed speaking to say, "We are holding the aircraft for some very special people who are on their way to the plane and the delay shouldn't be more than five minutes." The word came after waiting six times as long as we were promised that I was finally going to be on my way home. Why the hoopla over "these" folks?

I was expecting some celebrity or sport figure to be the reason for the hold up. Just get their butts in a seat and let's hit the gas I thought.

The attendant came back on the speaker to announce in a loud and excited voice that we were being joined by several U.S. Marines returning home from Iraq!

Just as they walked on board, the entire plane erupted into applause. The men were a bit taken by surprise by the 340 people cheering for them as they searched for their seats. They were having their hands shook and touched by almost everyone who was within an arm's distance from them as they passed down the aisle. One elderly woman kissed the hand of one of the Marines as he passed by her.

The applause, whistles and cheering didn't stop for a long time.

When we were finally airborne, I was not the only civilian checking his conscience as to the delays in "me" getting home, finding my easy chair, a cold beverage and the remote in my hand.

These men had done for all of us and I had been complaining silently about "me" and "my" issues I took for granted the everyday freedoms I enjoyed and the conveniences of the American way of life. I took for granted that others had paid the price for my ability to moan and complain about a few minutes delay to "me" while those Heroes were going home to their loved ones.

I attempted to get my selfish outlook back in order and minutes before we landed, I suggested to the attendant that she announce over the speaker a request for everyone to remain in their seats until our heroes were allowed to gather their things and be first off the plane.

The cheers and applause continued until the last Marine stepped off and we all rose to go about our too often taken for granted everyday freedoms. I felt proud of them.

I vowed that I will never forget that flight nor the lesson learned. I can't say it enough, THANK YOU to those Veterans and active servicemen and women who may read this and a prayer for those who cannot because they are no longer with us.

GOD BLESS AMERICA! WELCOME HOME AND THANKS FOR A JOB WELL DONE!!!

SNIFFER

A man sitting in an airliner, which is about to take off, when another man with a Labrador Retriever occupies the 2 seats besides him. The Lab is situated in the middle, and the first man is looking quizzically at the dog when the second man explains that they work for the airline. The airline rep said, "Don't mind Sniffer. He's a sniffing dog and he's the best there is. I'll show you once we get airborne when I put him to work."

The plane takes off and levels out when the handler says to the first man, "Watch this." He tells the dog, "Sniffer, search." Sniffer jumps down, walks along the aisle, and sits next to a woman for a few seconds. It then returns to its seat and puts one paw on the handler's arm. He says, "Good boy."

The airline rep turns to the first man and says, "That woman is in possession of marijuana, so I'm making a note of this and her seat number for the police who will apprehend her on arrival." "Fantastic!" replies the first man.

Once again he sends Sniffer to search the aisles, The Lab sniffs about, sits down beside a man for a few seconds, returns to its seat, and places two paws on the handler's arm. The airline rep says, "That man is carrying cocaine, so again I'm making a note of this and the seat number."

A third time the rep sends Sniffer to search the aisles. Sniffer goes up and down the plane and after a while sits down next to someone. He then comes racing back, jumps up onto his seat and craps a big pile. The first man is really grossed out by this behavior from a supposedly well-trained sniffing dog and asks, "What's the matter with this stupid dog?"

The handler nervously replies, "He just found a bomb."

MAXINE SPEAKS OUT
(Everyone knows this famous cartoon character)

- Maxine at the computer: "I keep hitting escape, but I'm still here."

- Some people can have all the lights on and still be in the dark.

- Dear Lord, I pray for: Wisdom, to understand a man, Love, to forgive him and, Patience, for his moods. Because, Lord, if I pray for strength, I'll just beat him to death.

- I'm out of bed and I made it to the keyboard. What more do you want.

- Got hooked up to high-speed internet. It crashes a lot faster now.

- On Labor Day, if one of my relatives sees a shadow, they all quit working for six weeks.

- Even doctors make mistakes. Mine asked me to undress.

- I find it helps to organize chores into categories: Things I won't do now; Things I won't do later; Things I'll never do.

- After you, celibacy seems attractive.

- If your friends can accurately guess your age, you need to find dumber friends.

- Don't like my attitude? Send me an email at: www.likeIcare.com.

- Don't let aging get you down. It's too hard to get back up!

- It's time to do some stuff around the house. Sit around it... walk around it...Lie around it....

- Here's a home remedy, Go Home. Hey, it'll make me feel better.

- Everything slows down with age, except the time it takes cake and ice cream to reach your hips.

- Age doesn't make you forgetful. Having way too many stupid things to remember makes you forgetful.

- Now that I'm older I thought it was great that I seemed to have more patients. Turns out that I just don't give a shit.

MORE REDNECK HUMOR

It is time to change from REDNECK humor to TRUE AMERICAN humor! Only I don't see it as humor, but the correct way to LIVE YOUR LIFE!

- You might be a TRUE AMERICAN if: It never occurred to you to be offended by the phrase "One nation, under God."

- You might be a TRUE AMERICAN if: You've never protested about seeing the Ten Commandments posted in public places.

- You might be a TRUE AMERICAN if: You still say "Christmas" instead of "Winter Festival."

- You might be a TRUE AMERICAN if: You bow your head when someone prays.

- You might be a TRUE AMERICAN if: You stand and place you hand over your heart when they play the National Anthem.

- You might be a TRUE AMERICAN if: You treat Vietnam Vets with great respect, and always have.

- You might be a TRUE AMERICAN if: You've never burned an American flag.

- You might be a TRUE AMERICAN if: You know what you believe and you aren't afraid to say so, not matter who is listening.

- You might be a TRUE AMERICAN if: You respect your elders and expect your kids to do the same.

- You might be a TRUE AMERICAN if: You'd give your last dollar to a friend.

ANOTHER HOLIDAY

Today is International Very Good Looking, Damn Smart Woman's Day, so please send this message to someone you think fits this description. Please do not send it back to me as I have already received it from a Very Good Looking, Damn Smart Woman! And remember this motto to live by: Life should NOT be a journey to the grave with the intention of arriving safely in an attractive and well preserved body, but rather to skid in sideways, chocolate in one hand, wine in the other, body thoroughly used up, totally worn out and screaming "WOO HOO what a ride!"

"You don't stop laughing when you get old; you get old when you stop laughing."

SURPRISING FACTS!

Captain Kangaroo passed away on January 23, 2004 at the age of 76, which is odd, because he always looked to be 76. (DOB 6/27/27). His death reminded me of the following story.

Some people have been a bit offended that the actor, Lee Marvin, is buried in a grave alongside 3 and 4 star generals at Arlington National Cemetery. His marker gives his name, rank (PVT) and service (USMC). Nothing else. Here's a guy who was only a famous movie star who served his time, why the heck does he rate burial with these guys? Well, following is the amazing answer: I always liked Lee Marvin, but didn't know the extent of his Corps experience.

In a time when many Hollywood stars served their country in the armed forces often in real echelon posts where they were carefully protected, only to be trotted out to perform for the cameras in war bond promotions, Lee Marvin was a genuine hero. He won the Navy Cross at Iwo Jima. There is only one higher Naval award…the Medal of Honor. If that is a surprising comment on the true character of the man, he credits his sergeant with an even greater show of bravery.

Dialog form "The Tonight Show with Johnny Carson": His guest was Lee Marvin. Johnny said, "Lee, I'll bet a lot of people are unaware that you were a Marine in the initial landing at Iwo Jima … and that during the course of that action you earned the Navy Cross and were severely wounded."

"Yeah, yeah…I got shot square in the bottom and they gave me the Cross for securing a hot spot about halfway up Suribachi. Bad thing about getting shot up on a mountain is guys getting shot hauling you down. But, Johnny, at Iwo I served under the bravest man I ever knew…. We both got the Cross the same day, but what he did for his Cross made mine look cheap in comparison. That dumb guy actually stood up on Red Beach and directed his troops to move forward and get the hell off the beach. Bullets flying by, with mortar rounds landing everywhere and he stood there as the main target of gunfire so that he could get his men to safety. He did this on more than one occasion because his men's safety was more important than his own life.

"That Sergeant and I have been lifelong friends. When they brought me off Suribachi we passed the Sergeant and he lit a smoke and passed it to me, lying on my belly on the litter and said, 'where'd they get you Lee?' Well Bob … if you make it home before me, tell Mom to sell the outhouse!

"Johnny, I'm not lying, Sergeant Keeshan was the bravest man I ever knew. The Sergeant's name is Bob Keeshan. You and the world know him as Captain Kangaroo."

On another note, there was this wimpy little man (who just passed away) on PBS, gentle and quiet. Mr. Rogers is another of those you would least suspect of being anything but what he now portrays to our youth. But Mr. Rogers was a U.S. Navy Seal, combat-proven in Vietnam with over twenty-five confirmed kills to his name. He wore a long-sleeved sweater on TV, to cover the many tattoos on his forearm and biceps. He was a master in small arms and hand-to-hand combat, able to disarm or kill in a heartbeat.

After the war Mr. Rogers became an ordained Presbyterian minister and therefore a pacifist. Vowing to never harm another human and also dedicating the rest of his life to trying to help lead children on the right path in life. He hid away the tattoos and his past life and won our hearts with his quiet wit and charm.

America's real heroes don't flaunt what they did; they quietly go about their day-to-day lives, doing what they do best. They earned our respect and the freedoms that we all enjoy.

Look around and see if you can find one of those heroes in your midst. Often, they are the ones you'd least suspect, but would most like to have on your side if anything ever happened. Take the time to thank anyone that has fought for our freedom. With encouragement they could be the next Captain Kangaroo or Mr. Rogers.

TALIBAN MESSAGE

This morning, from a cave somewhere in Pakistan, Taliban Minister of Migration, Mohammed Omar, warned the United States that if military action against Iraq continues, Taliban authorities will cut off America's supply of convenience store managers. And if this action does not yield sufficient results, cab drivers will be next, followed by Dell customer service reps.

This is getting ugly.

NEW SUPERMARKET TECHNOLOGY

The new supermarket near our house has an automatic water mister to keep the produce fresh. Just before it goes on, you hear the sound of distant thunder and the smell of fresh rain.

When you approach the milk case, you hear cows mooing and witness the scent of fresh hay.

When you approach the egg case, you hear hens cluck and cackle and the air is filled with the pleasing aroma of bacon and eggs frying.

The veggie department features the smell of fresh buttered corn.

I don't buy toilet paper there anymore.

ASSES

Life is all about ass; you are either covering it, laughing it off, kicking it, kissing it, busting it, trying to get a piece of it, behaving like one, or you live with one!!!

CLASSIC RESPONSES

If you remember The Original Hollywood Squares and its comics, this will bring tears to your eyes. These great questions and answers are from the days when Hollywood Squares game show responses were spontaneous and clever, not scripted and (often) dull as they are now. Peter Marshall was the host asking the questions, of course.

Q: Do female frogs croak?
A: Paul Lynde – If you hold their little heads under water long enough.

Q: If you're going to make a parachute jump, at least how high should you be?
A: Charley Weaver – Three days of steady drinking should do it.

Q: True or False, a pea can last as long as 5,000 years.
A: George Gobel – Boy, it sure seems that way sometimes.

Q: You've been having trouble going to sleep. Are you probably man or a woman?
A: Don Knotts – That's what's been keeping me awake.

Q: According to Cosmo, if you meet a stranger at a party and you think that he is attractive, is it okay to come out and ask him if he's married?
A: Rose Marie – No, wait until morning.

Q: Which of your five senses tends to diminish as you get older?
A: Charley Weaver – My sense of decency.

Q: In Hawaiian, does it take more than three words to say "I Love You"?
A: Vincent Price – No, you can say it with a pineapple and a twenty.

Q: What are "Do It"; "I Can Help"; and "I Can't Get Enough"?
A: George Goble – I don't know, but it's coming from the next apartment.

Q: As you grow older, do you tend to gesture more or less with your hands while talking?
A: Rose Marie – You ask me one more growing old question Peter, and I'll give you a gesture you'll never forget.

Q: Paul, why do Hell's Angels wear leather?
A: Paul Lynde – Because chiffon wrinkles too easily.

Q: Charley, you've just decided to grow strawberries. Are you growing to get any during the first year?
A: Charley Weaver – Of course not, I'm too busy growing strawberries.

Q: In bowling, what's a perfect score?
A: Rose Marie – Ralph, the pin boy.

Q: It is considered in bad taste to discuss two subjects at nudist camps. One is politics, what is the other?
A: Tape measures.

Q: During a tornado, are you safer in the bedroom or in the closet?
A: Rose Marie – Unfortunately Peter, I'm always safe in the bedroom.

Q: Can boys join the Campfire Girls?
A: Marty Allen – Only after lights out.

Q: When you pat a dog on its head he will wag his tail. What will a goose do?
A: Paul Lynde – Make him bark?

Q: If you were pregnant for two years, what would you give birth to?
A: Paul Lynde – Whatever it is, it would never be afraid of the dark.

Q: According to Ann Landers, is there anything wrong with getting into the habit of kissing a lot of people?
A: Charley Weaver – It got me out of the army.

Q: It is the most abused and neglected part of your body, what is it?
A: Paul Lynde – Mine may be abused but it certainly isn't neglected.

Q: Back in the old days, when Great Grandpa put horseradish on his head, what was he trying to do?
A: George Gobel – Get it in his mouth.

Q: Who stays pregnant for a longer period of time, your wife or your elephant?
A: Paul Lynde – Who told you about my elephant?

Q: When a couple has a baby, who is responsible for its sex?
A: Charley Weaver – I'll lend him the car; the rest is up to him.

Q: Jackie Gleason recently revealed that he firmly believes in them and has actually seen them on at least two occasions. What are they?
A: Charley Weaver – His feet.

Q: According to Ann Landers, what are two things you should never do in bed?
A: Paul Lynde – Point and laugh.

ITALIAN COOKIES

This is for all the Italians out there, and those who are lucky enough to be married to and Italian, and even to all friends of Italians.

An elderly Italian man lay dying in his bed. While suffering the agonies of impending death, he suddenly smelled the aroma of his favorite Italian anisette sprinkle cookies wafting up the stairs. Gathering his remaining strength, he lifted himself from the bed. Leaning against the wall, he slowly made his way out of the bedroom, and with even greater effort, griping the railing with both hands he crawled downstairs. With labored breath, he leaned against the doorframe, gazing into the kitchen.

Where if not for death's agony, he would have thought himself already in heaven. For there, spread out upon waxed paper on the kitchen table were literally hundreds of his favorite anisette sprinkled cookies. Was it heaven? Or was it one final act of heroic love from his devoted Italian wife of sixty years, seeing to it that he left this world a happy man?

Mustering one great final effort, he threw himself towards the table, landing on his knees in a crumpled posture. His parched lips parted, the wondrous taste of the cookie was already in his mouth, seemingly bringing him back to life.

The aged and withered hand trembled on its way to a cookie at the edge of the table, when it was suddenly smacked with a spatula by his wife.

"Get out of here!" she shouted, "There're for the funeral."

MESSAGE TO OSAMA BIN LADEN

Osama Bin Laden, your time is short; We'd rather you die, than come to court. Why are you hiding if it was in God's name? You're just a punk with a turban; a pathetic shame.

I have a question, about your theory and laws; "How come you never die for the cause?" Is it because you're a coward who counts on others? Well, here in America, we stand by our brothers.

As is usual, you failed in your mission; If you expected pure chaos, you can keep on wishing Americans are now focused and stronger than ever; Your death has become our next endeavor.

What you tried to kill, doesn't live in our walls; It's not in buildings or shopping malls.

If all of our structures came crashing down; It would still be there, safe and sound. Because pride and courage can't be destroyed; Even if the towers leave a deep void.

We'll band together and fill the holes. We'll bury our dead and bless their souls. But then our energy will focus on you; And you'll feel the wrath of the Red, White and Blue.

So slither and hide like a snake in the grass; Because America's coming to kick your ass!

MY CANDIDATE FOR PRESIDENT IN 2008

Here we are already discussing the future President of the United States in the year 2008. Well, I have my own candidate and I'm sure that once you know who I'm voting for, you will also agree.

For those of you how would like another choice for President, I have the best solution: It is probably time we have a woman as President. My choice, and I hope yours as well, is a very special lady who has all the answers to our problems.

PLEASE give it a thought when you have a moment...MAXINE FOR PRESIDENT!!!

Maxine: "It's...one nation UNDER GOD..., or bite my skinny old ass and leave!"

Maxine: "If you MUST burn our flag, please wrap yourself in it first."

Very eloquently put...don't you think?

Maxine on "Driver Safety": "I can't use the cell phone in the car. I have to keep my hands free for making gestures."

Maxine on "Housework": "I do my housework in the nude. It gives me an incentive to clean the mirrors as quickly as possible."

Maxine on "Lawn Care": "The key to a nice-looking lawn is a good mower. I recommend one who is muscular and shirtless."

Maxine on "The Perfect Man": "All I'm looking for is a guy who'll do what I want, when I want, for as long as I want, and then go away. Or wait nearby, like Dust Buster, charged up and ready when needed."

Maxine on "Technology Revolution": "My idea of rebooting is kicking somebody in the butt twice."

Maxine on "Aging": "Take every birthday with a grain of salt. This works much better if the salt accompanies a Margarita."

I'm telling you...she's the perfect candidate. So don't forget, November 2008: VOTE FOR MAXINE FOR PRESIDENT OF THE UNITED STATES. There's no one better for the job.

NOAH'S SECOND ARK

In the year 2006, the Lord came unto Noah, who was now living in the United States, and said, "Once again, the earth has become wicked and overpopulated, and I see the end of all flesh before me. Build another Ark and save 2 of every living thing along with a few good humans." He gave Noah the blueprints, saying, "You have 6 months to build the Ark before I will start the unending rain for 40 days and 40 nights."

Six months later, the Lord looked down and saw Noah weeping in his yard but no Ark. "Noah!" he roared, "I'm about to start the rain! Where is the Ark?"

"Forgive me, Lord," begged Noah, "but things have changed. I needed a building permit. I've been arguing with the inspector about the need for a sprinkler system. My neighbors claim that I've violated the neighborhood zoning laws by building the Ark in my yard and exceeding the height limitations. We have to go to the Development Appeal Board for a decision.

"Then the Department of Transportation demanded a bond be posted for the future costs of moving power lines and other overhead obstructions, to clear the passage for the Ark's move to the sea. I told them that the sea would be coming to us, but they wouldn't hear nothing of it.

"Getting the wood was another problem. There's a ban on cutting local trees in order to save the spotted owl. I tried to convince the environmentalists that I needed the wood to save the owls - - but no go!

"When I started gathering the animals, I got sued by an animal rights group. They insisted that I was confining wild animals against their will. They argued the accommodations were too restrictive, and it was cruel and inhumane to put so many animals in a confided space.

"Then the EPA ruled that I couldn't build the Ark until they'd conducted an environmental impact study on your proposed flood.

"I'm still trying to resolve a complaint with the Human Rights Commission on how many minorities I'm supposed to hire for my building crew.

"Immigration and Naturalization is checking the green-card status of most of the people who want to work. The trades unions say I can't use my sons. They insist I have to hire only Union workers with Ark-building experience.

"To make matters worse, the IRS seized all my assets, claiming I'm trying to leave the country illegally with endangered species.

"So, forgive me, Lord, but it would take at least 10 years for me to finish this Ark."

Suddenly the skies cleared, the sun began to shine, and a rainbow stretched across the sky. Noah looked up in wonder and asked, "You mean you're not going to destroy the world?"

"No," said the Lord. "The government beat me to it."

EVOLUTION OF MATH

Last week I purchased a burger and fries at McDonalds for $3.58.

The counter girl took my $4.00 and I pulled 8 cents from my pocket and gave it to her. She stood there, holding the nickel and 3 pennies. While looking at the screen on her register, I sensed her discomfort and tried to tell her just to give me two quarters, but she hailed the manager for help. While he tried to explain the transaction to her, she stood there and cried.

Why do I tell you this? Because of the evolution in teaching math since the 1950's.

Teaching math in 1950. A logger sells a truckload of lumber for $100. His cost of production is 4/5 of the price. What is his profit?

Teaching math in 1960. A logger sells a truckload of lumber for $100. His cost of production is 4/5 of the price, or $80.00. What is his profit?

Teaching math in 1970. A logger sells a truckload of lumber for $100. His cost is $80. Did he make a profit?

Teaching math in 1980. A logger sells a truckload of lumber for $100. his cost of production is $80 and his profit is $20. Your assignment: Underline the number 20.

Teaching math in 1990. A logger cuts down a beautiful forest because he is selfish and inconsiderate and cares nothing for the habitat of animals or the preservation of our woodlands. He does this so he can make a profit of $20. What do you think of this way of making a living? Topic for class participation after answering the question: How did the birds and squirrels feel as the logger cut down their homes? (There are no wrong answers.)

Teaching math in 2006. Un ranchero vende una carreta de Madera por$100. El costo de produccion es $80. Cuantos tortillas se puede comprar?

DARK IN HERE

A woman takes a lover home during the day while her husband is at work. Her 9-year-old son comes home unexpectedly, sees them and hides in the bedroom closet to watch. The woman's husband also comes home. She puts her lover in the closet, not realizing that the little boy is in there already.

The little boys says, "Dark in here."

The man says, "Yes, it is."

Boy - "I have a baseball."

Man - "That's nice."

Boy - "Want to buy it?"

Man - "No, thanks."

Boy - "My dad's outside."

Man - "OK, how much?"

Boy - "$250."

In the next few weeks, it happens again that the boy and the lover are in the closet together.

Boy - "Dark in here."

Man - "Yes, it is."

Boy - "I have a baseball glove."

The lover, remembering the last time, asks the boy, "How much?"

Boy - $750."

Man - "Sold."

A few days later, the father says to the boy, "Grab your glove, let's go outside and have a game of catch."

The boy says, "I can't, I sold my baseball and my glove."

The father says, "How much did you sell them for?"

Boy - "$1,000."

The father says, "That's terrible to overcharge your friends like that! ...that is way more than those two things cost. I'm going to take you to church and make you confess."

They go to the church and the father makes the little boy sit in the confession booth and he closes the door.

The boy says, "Dark in here."

The priest says, "Don't start that shit again, you're in my closet now."

TRICK QUESTION

This is not a trick question. It is as it reads. No one I know has gotten it right.

A woman, while at the funeral of her own mother, met a gay guy whom she did not know. She thought this guy was amazing. She believed him to be her dream guy so much that she fell in love with him right there, but never asked for his number and could not find him. A few days later she killed her sister.

Question: What is her motive for killing her sister?

Give this some thought before you answer, the answer is below.

Answer: She was hoping the guy would appear at the funeral again. If you answered this correctly, you think like a psychopath. This was a test by a famous American Psychologist used to test if one has the same mentality as a killer.

Many arrested serial killers took part in the test and answered the question correctly.

If you didn't answer the question correctly, good for you.

If you got the answer correct, please let me know so I can take you off my email list. Thanks.

WHY WE SPLIT-UP

She told me we couldn't afford beer anymore and I'd have to quit.
Then I caught her spending:
$65.00 on make-up,
$165.00 for a cut & color,
$30.00 for a manicure,
$40.00 for a pedicure,
$50.00 on vitamins,
$300.00 on clothes,
and $600.00 for a gym membership.
I asked how come I had to give up stuff and not her. She said she needed it to look pretty for me.
I told her that was what the beer was for. I don't think she's coming back.

MONASTERY LIFE

A young monk arrives at the monastery. He is assigned to helping the other monks in copying the old canons and laws of the church my hand.

He notices, however, that all of the monks are copying from copies, not from the original manuscript. So, the new monk goes to the head abbot to question this, pointing out that if someone made even a small error in the first copy, it would never be picked up! In fact, that error would be continued in all of the subsequent copies.

The head monk, says, "We have been copying from the copies for centuries, but you make a good point my son."

He goes down into the dark caves underneath the monastery where the original manuscripts are held as archives in a locked vault that hasn't been opened for hundreds of years. Hours go by and nobody sees the old abbot.

So, the young monk gets worried and goes down to look for him. He sees him banging his head against the wall and wailing, "We missed the 'R'!, we missed the 'R!'"

His forehead is all bloody and bruised and he is crying uncontrollably. The young monk asks the old abbot, "What's wrong, father?"

With a choking voice, the old abbot replies, "The word was... CELEBRATE!!!"

ARE YOU A DEMOCRAT,
A REPUBLICAN, OR A REDNECK?

Here is a little test that will help you decide.

You're walking down a deserted street with your wife and two small children. Suddenly, an Islamic terrorist with a huge knife comes around the corner, locks eyes with you, screams obscenities, praises Allah, raises the knife, and charges at you.

You are carrying a Glock cal. 40, and you are an expert shot. You have mere seconds before he reaches you and your family.

What do you do?

Democrat's answer:
Well, that's not enough information to answer the question! Does the man look poor or oppressed? Have I ever done anything to him that would inspire him to attack? Could we run away? What does my wife think? What about the kids? Could I possibly swing the gun like a club and knock the knife out of his hand? What does the law say about this situation? Does the Glock have appropriate safety built into it? Why am I carrying a loaded gun anyway, and what kind of message does this sent to society and to my children? Is it possible he'd be happy with just killing me? Does he definitely want to kill me, or would he be content just to wound me? If I were to grab his knees and hold on, could my family get away while he was stabbing me? Should I call 9-1-1? Why is this street so deserted? We need to raise taxes, have a paint and weed day and make this a happier, healthier street that would discourage such behavior. This is all so confusing! I need to discuss with some friends over a latte' and try to come to a consensus.

Republican's Answer:
BANG!

Redneck's Answer:
BANG! BANG! BANG! BANG! BANG! BANG! BANG! BANG!
BANG! Click…(sounds of reloading)
BANG! BANG! BANG! BANG! BANG! BANG! BANG! BANG!
BANG!

Daughter: Nice grouping, Daddy! Were those the Winchester Silver Tips or Hollow Points?"

Son: "You got him, Pop! Can I shoot the next one?"

Wife: "You are NOT taking that to the taxidermist!

It's good to be a redneck!!!!

WINDOWS 2006 SOUTHERN EDITION

Dear Customers:

It has come to our attention that a few copies of the **Windows 2006 Southern Edition** may have accidentally been shipped outside of the south. If you have one of these, you may need help understanding the commands. The **Southern Edition** may be recognized by the unique opening screen. It reads: **Winders 2006**, with a background picture of Waylan and Willie superimposed on a bottle of Jim Beam.

Please also note: The Recycle Bin is labeled "Outhouse."

My Computer is called **"This Dern Contraption."**
Dial Up Networking is called **"Good Ol' Boys."**
Control Panel is known as **"The Dashboard."**
Hard Drive is referred to as **"4-Wheel Drive."**
Floppies are **"Them little ol' plastic thangs."**
Instead of an error message, **"Duct tape"** pops up.

Changes in Terminology in **Southern Edition**:
Cancel................stopdat
Reset.................try'er agin
Yes...................yep
No....................nope
Find..................hunt fer it
Go To.................over yonder
Back..................back yonder
Help..................hep me out here
Stop..................kwitt (WHOA!)
Start.................crank'er up
Settings.............settins

Programs............stuff at duz stuff
Documents..........stuff ah done did

Also note that **Southern Edition** does not recognize capital letters or punctuation marks. Some programs that are exclusive to **Winders 2006**:

Tiperiter..................a word processing program
Colerin' Book............ A graphics program
Cyferin' Mersheen.......calculator
Outhouse Paper..........notepad
Inner-net..................Microsoft explorer 5.0
Pichers....................a graphic viewer

We regret any inconvenience it may have caused. If you received a copy of the **Southern Edition**, you may return it to Microsoft for a replacement version.

FATHER

A guy goes to a supermarket and notices a beautiful blond wave at him and says hello. He's rather taken back, because he can't place where he knows her from, so he says, "do you know me?" to which she replies, "I think you're the father of one of my kids."

Now he thinks back to the only time he has ever been unfaithful to his wife and says, "My God, are you the stripper from my bachelor party that I laid on the pool table with all my buddies watching, while your partner whipped my butt with wet celery and then stuck a carrot up my butt?"

She said, "No, I'm your son's math teacher."

RETIREMENT AND GOLF

Dear Fellow Golfing Buddies,

It is important for men to remember that, as women grow older, it becomes harder for them to maintain the same quality of housekeeping as when they were younger. When you notice this, try not to yell at them. Some are oversensitive, and there's nothing worse than an oversensitive woman.

My name is Jim. In order to help you with this problem let me relate how I handled the situation with my wife, Peggy. When I retired a few years ago, it became necessary for Peggy to get a full-time job along with her part-time job, both for the extra income and for the health benefits that we needed.

Shortly after she started working that extra job, I noticed she was beginning to show she age. I usually get home from the golf course about the same time she gets home from work so I see her in the natural light where it is really noticeable.

Although she knows how hungry I am, she almost always says she has to rest for half an hour or so before she starts dinner. I don't yell at her. Instead, I tell her to take her time and just wake me when she gets dinner on the table. I generally have lunch in the Men's Grill at the club so eating out is not reasonable. I'm ready for some home-cooked grub when I hit the door. She used to do the dishes as soon as we finished eating. But now it's not unusual for them to sit on the table for several hours after dinner. I do what I can by diplomatically reminding her several times each evening that they won't clean themselves. I know she really appreciates this, as it does seem to motivate her to get them done before she goes to bed.

Another symptom of aging is complaining, I think. For example, she will say that it is difficult for her to find time to pay the monthly bills during her lunch hour. But, boys, we take 'em for better or worse, so I just smile and offer encouragement. I tell her to stretch it out over two or even three days. That way she won't have to rush so much. I also remind her that missing lunch won't have to rush so much. I also remind her that missing lunch completely now and then wouldn't hurt her any (if you know what I mean). I like to think tact is one of my strong points.

When doing simple jobs, she seems to think she needs more rest periods. She had to take a break when she was only half finished mowing the yard. I try not to make a scene. I'm a fair man. I tell her to fix herself a nice, ole cold glass of freshly squeezed lemonade and just sit for a while. And, as long as she is making one for herself, she may as will make one for me too.

I know that I probably look like a saint in the way I support Peggy. I'm not saying that showing this much consideration is easy. I understand that many men will find it difficult. Some will find it impossible! Nobody knows better than I do how frustrating women get as they get older. However, guys, even if you just use a little more tact and less criticism of your aging wife because of this article, then I will consider that writing it was well worthwhile. After all my good buddies, we are put on this earth to help each other.

Sincerely,
Jim

Editor's Note:
Jim died suddenly on August 27 of a perforated rectum. The police report says he was found with a Calloway extra long 50-inch Big Bertha Driver II golf club jammed up his rear-end, with less than 5

inches of the John Daly "Grip it n' Rip it" signature grip showing. A sledge hammer lying nearby was suspected as possibly implicit.

His wife Peggy was arrested and charged with murder. However, at the trial, the 9-woman, 2-metrosexual, 1 Gayboy jury took only 15 minutes to find her Not Guilty. Having heard the testimony of Jim's tactful conduct since his retirement, they completely accepted her defense that Jim somehow, without looking, had tripped over his sledge hammer and accidentally sat down on his golf club.

OBITUARY

Today we remember the passing of a beloved old friend, Mr. Common Sense. Mr. Sense had been with us for many years. No one knows for sure how old he was since his birth records were long ago lost in bureaucratic red tape.

He will be remembered as having cultivated such valuable lessons as knowing when to come in out of the rain, why the early birds gets the worm and that life isn't always fair. Common Sense lived by simple, sound financial policies (don't spend more than you earn) and reliable parenting strategies (adults, no kids, are in charge).

His health began to rapidly deteriorate when well-intentioned but overbearing regulations were set in place. Reports of a six-year old boy charged with sexual harassment for kissing a classmate; teens suspended from school for using mouthwash after lunch; and a teacher fired for reprimanding an unruly student, only worsened his condition.

Mr. Sense declined even further when schools were required to get parental consent to administer aspirin to a student; but could not inform the parents when a student became pregnant and wanted to have an abortion.

Finally, Common Sense lost the will to live as the Ten Commandments became contraband; churches became businesses; and criminals received better treatment than their victims.

Common Sense finally gave up the ghost after a woman failed to realize that a steaming cup of coffee was hot. She spilled a bit in her lap, and was awarded a huge financial settlement.

Common Sense was preceded in death by his parents, Truth and Trust, his wife, Discretion; his daughter Responsibility; and his son, Reason. He is survived by two stepbrothers; My Rights and Ima Whiner.

Not many attended his funeral because so few realized he was gone.

If you remember him, pass this on; if not, join the majority and do nothing.

NO JOKE

Because of recent abductions in daylight hours, refresh yourself of these things to do in an emergency situation... This is you to share with your spouse, your children and everyone you know.

1. Tip from Tae Kwon Do: The elbow is the strongest point on your body. If you are close enough to use it, do!

2. Learned this from a tourist guide in New Orleans. If a robber asks for your wallet and/or purse, Do Not Hand It To Him. Toss it away from you...chances are that he is more interested in your wallet and/or purse than you, and he will go for the wallet/purse. Then run like mad in the other direction.

3. If you are ever thrown into the trunk of a car, kick out the back tail lights and stick your arm out the hole and start waving like crazy. The driver won't see you, but everybody else will. This has saved lives.

4. Women have a tendency to get into their cars after shopping, eating, working, etc, and just sit (doing their checkbook or making a list, etc. Don't Do This! The predator will be watching you, and this is the perfect opportunity for him to get in on the passenger side, put a gun to your head, and tell you where to go. As soon as you get into your car, lock the doors and leave.

5. If someone is in the car with a gun to your head, Do Not Drive Off, repeat: Do Not Drive Off. Instead gun the engine and speed into anything, wrecking the car. Your Air Bag will save you. If the person is in the back seat, they will get the worst of it. As soon as the car crashes, bail out and run. It is better than having them find your body in a remote location.

6. A few notes about getting into your car in a parking lot, or parking garage: A.) Be aware: look around you, look into your car, at the passenger side floor, and in the back seat, B.) If are parking next to a big van, enter your car from the passenger door. Most serial killers attack their victims by pulling them into their vans while the women are attempting to get into their cars, C.) Look at the car parked on the driver's side of your vehicle, and the passenger side. If a male is sitting alone in the seat nearest your car, you may want to walk back into the mall, or work, and get a guard/policeman to walk you back out. It is always better to be safe than sorry. (And better paranoid than dead.)

7. Always take the elevator instead of the stairs. (Stairwells are horrible places to be alone and the perfect crime spot.)

8. If the predator has a gun and you are not under his control, Always Run! The predator will only hit you (a running target is harder to hit). The zig-zag pattern is preferred!

9. Women are always trying to be sympathetic: Stop. Being sympathetic may get you raped, or killed. Ted Bundy, the serial killer was a good looking guy, well educated, and always played on the sympathy of unsuspecting women. He walked with a cane, or a limp, and often asked "for help" into his vehicle which is when he abducted his next victim.

10. Someone told me that her friend heard a crying baby on her porch and she called the police because it was late and she thought it was weird. The police told her "Whatever You Do, DO NOT Open Your Door."

CAREFUL WHAT YOU WISH FOR

A married couple in their early 60's was out celebrating their 35th anniversary in a quiet, romantic little restaurant. Suddenly, a tiny beautiful fairy appeared on their table and said, "For being such an exemplary married couple and for being so faithful to each other for all this time, I will grant you each a wish."

"Oh, I want to travel around the world with my darling husband" said the wife. The fairy waved her magic wand and poof-two tickets for the Queen Mary II luxury liner appeared in her hands.

Then it was the husband's turn. He thought for a moment and said, "Well, this is all very romantic, but an opportunity like this will never come again. I'm sorry my love, but my wish is to have a wife 30 years younger than me."

The wife and fairy were deeply disappointed, but a wish is a wish. So the fairy waved her magic wand and poof! The husband became 92 years old. Men who are ungrateful should remember, fairies are female.

CHEMISTRY EXAM

The following is supposedly an actual question given on a chemistry mid-term: The answer by one student was so 'profound" that the professor shared it with colleagues, via the Internet, which is, of course, why we now have the pleasure of enjoying it as well.

Bonus Question: Is Hell exothermic (gives off heat) or endothermic (absorbs heat)?

Most of the students wrote proofs of their beliefs using Boyle' Law (gas cools when it expands and heats when it is compressed) or some variant.

One student, however, wrote the following: First, we need to know how the mass of Hell is changing in time. So we need to know the rate at which souls are moving into Hell and the rate which they are leaving. I think that we can safely assume that once a soul gets to Hell, it will not leave. Therefore, no souls are leaving. As for how many souls are entering? Hell, let's look at the different Religions that exist in the world today. Most of these religions state that if you are not a member of their religion, you will go to Hell. Since there is more than one of these religions and since people do not belong to more than one religion's, we can project that all souls go to Hell. With birth and death rates as they are, we can expect the number of souls in Hell to increase exponentially.

Now we look at the rate of change of the volume in Hell, because Boyle's Law states that in order for the temperature and pressure in Hell to stay the same, the volume of Hell has to expand proportionately as souls are added. This gives two possibilities: 1. If Hell is expanding at a slower rate than the rate at which souls enter

Hell, then the temperature and pressure in Hell will increase until all Hell breaks loose. 2. If Hell is expanding at a rate faster than the increase of souls in Hell, then the temperature and pressure will and pressure will drop until Hell freezes over. So which is it?

If we accept the postulate given to me by Teresa during my Freshman year that, "it will be a cold day in Hell before I sleep with you," and take into account that the fact that I slept with her last night, then number 2 must be true, and thus I am sure that Hell is exothermic and has already frozen over.

The corollary of this theory is that since Hell has frozen over, it follows that it is not accepting any more souls and is therefore, extinct, leaving only Heaven thereby proving the existence of a divine being which explains why, last night, Teresa kept shouting "Oh my God."

PONDERABLES

How important does a person have to be before they are considered assassinated instead of just murdered?

- If money doesn't grow on trees, then why do banks have branches?

- Since bread is square, then why is sandwich meat round?

- Why do you have to "put your two cents in"…but it's only a "penny for your thoughts?" Where's that extra penny going?

- Once you're in heaven, do you get stuck wearing the clothes you were buried in for eternity?

- Why does a round pizza come is a square box?

- What disease did cured ham actually have?

- How is it that we put a man on the moon before we figured out it would be a good idea to put wheels on luggage?

- Why is it that people say they "slept like a baby" when babies wake up like every two hours?

- If a deaf person has to go to court, is it still called a hearing?

- Why are you "IN" a movie, but you're "ON TV"?

- Why do people pay to go up tall buildings and then put money in binoculars to look at things on the ground?

- How come we choose from just two people for President and fifty for Miss America?

- Why do doctors leave the room while you change? They're going to see you naked anyway.

- If a 911 operator has a heart attack, whom does he/she call?

- Why is "bra" singular and "panties" plural?

- Do illiterate people get the full effect of Alphabet soup?

- Who was the first person to look at a cow and say, "I think I'll squeeze these dangly things here, and drink whatever comes out!"

- Or watch a white thing come out a chicken's behind and think, "that ought to taste good."

- Why do toasters always have a setting that burns the toast to a horrible crisp, which no decent human being would eat?

- Why is there a light in the fridge and not in the freezer?

- When your photo is taken for your driver's license, why do they tell you to smile? If you are stopped by the police and asked for your license, are you going to be smiling?

- If Jimmy cracks corn and no one cares, why is there a stupid song about him?

- Can a hearse carrying a corpse drive in the carpool lane?

- If the professor of Gilligan's Island can make a radio out of a coconut, why can't he fix a hole in a boat?

- Why do people point to their wrist when asking for the time, but don't point to their crotch when they ask where the bathroom is?

- Why does Goofy stand erect while Pluto remains on all fours? They're both dogs!

- What do you call male ballerinas?

- Can blind people see their dreams? Do they dream?

- If Wyle E. Coyote had enough money to buy all that ACME crap, why didn't he just buy dinner?

- If corn oil is made from corn, and vegetables oil is made from vegetables, what is baby oil made from?

- If electricity comes from electrons, does morality come from morons?

- Is Disney World the only people trap operated by a mouse?

- Do the Alphabet song and Twinkle, Twinkle Little Star have the same tune?

- Why did you just try singing the two songs above?

- Why do they call it an asteroid when it's outside the hemisphere, but call it a hemorrhoid when it's in your butt?

- Did you ever notice that when you blow in a dog's face, he gets mad at you, but when you take him for a car ride he sticks his head out the window?

HOW THE "LEFT" STOLE CHRISTMAS

Twas the month before Christmas
When all through the land,
Not a Christian was praying
Nor taking a stand.
See the PC Police had taken away,
The reason for Christmas – no one could say.
The children were told by their schools not to sing,
About Shepherds and Wise Men and Angels and things.
It might hurt people's feelings, the teachers would say
December 25th is just a "Holiday."
Yet the shoppers were ready with cash, checks and credit
Pushing folks down to the floor just to get it!
CD's from Madonna, an X Box, an I-Pod
Something was changing, something quite odd!
Retailers promoted Ramadan and Kwanzaa
In hopes to sell books by Franken & Fonda.
As Targets were hanging their trees upside down
At Lowe's the word Christmas – was nowhere to be found.
At K-Mart and Staples and Penny's and Sears
You won't hear the word Christmas; it won't touch your ears.
Inclusive, sensitive, Di-ver-si-ty
Are words that were used to intimidate me.
Now Daschle, Now Darden, Now Sharpton, Wolf Blitzen
On Boxer, on Rather, on Kerry, on Clinton!
At the top of the Senate, there arose such a clatter
To eliminate Jesus, in all public matter.
And we spoke not a word, as they took away our faith
Forbidden to speak of salvation and grace
The true gift of Christmas was exchanged and discarded
The reason for the season, stopped before it started.

So as you celebrate "Winter Break" under your "Dream Tree"
Sipping your Starbucks, listen to me.
Choose your words carefully, choose what you say
Shout MERRY CHRISTMAS, not Happy Holiday!

CORPORATE DIVERSITY

Recently, a large corporation hired several cannibals to increase their diversity.

"You are all part of our team now," said the Human resources rep during the welcoming briefing. "You get all the usual benefits and you can go to the cafeteria for something to eat, but please do not eat any employees." The cannibals promised they would not.

Four weeks later their boss remarked, "You're all working very hard and I'm satisfied with your work. We have noticed a marked increase in the whole company's performance. However, one of our secretaries had disappeared. Do any of you know what happened to her?

The cannibals all shook their heads, No.

After the boss had left, the leader of the cannibals said to the others, "Which one of you idiots ate the secretary?" A hand rose hesitantly.

"You fool!" the leader continued. "For four weeks we've been eating managers and no one noticed anything BUT Nooooooo, you had to go and eat someone who actually does something around here."

REDNECK LOVE POEM

Susie Lee done fell in love;
She planned to marry Joe
She was so happy 'bout it all
She told her pappy so.

Pappy told her, "Susie gal,
You'll have to find another.
I'd just as soon yo' Ma don't know,
But Joe is yo' half brother."

So Susie put aside her Joe
And planned to marry Will.
But after telling pappy this,
He said, "There's trouble still.

You can't marry Will, my gal,
And please don't tell you' mother,
But Will and Joe, and several Mo'
I know is you' half brother."

But mama knew and said, "My child,
Just do what makes yo' happy.
Marry Will or Marry Joe.
You ain't no kin to pappy."

BRAIN CRAMPS

On September 17, 1994, Alabama's Heather Whitestone was selected as Miss America 1995. Question: If you could live forever, would you and why? Answer: "I would not live forever, because we should not live forever, because it we were supposed to live forever, then we would live forever, but we cannot live forever, which is why I would not live forever."

"Whenever I watch TV and see those poor starving kids all over the world, I can't help but cry. I mean I'd love to be skinny like that, but not with all those flies and death and stuff." --Mariah Carey –

"Smoking kills. If you're killed, you've lost a very important part of your life." -- Brooke Shields, during an interview to become Spokesperson for federal anti-smoking campaign.—

"I've never had major knee surgery on any other part of my body." -- Winston Bennett, University of Kentucky basketball forward.—

"Outside of the killings, Washington has one of the lowest crime rates in the country." –Mayor Marion Berry, Washington, DC—

"I'm not going to have some reporters pawing through our papers. We are the President." --Hillary Clinton, commenting on the release of subpoenaed documents.—

"That lowdown scoundrel deserves to be kicked to death by a jackass, and I'm just that one to do it," -- A congressional candidate in Texas.
—

"Half this game is ninety percent mental." --Philadelphia Phillies manager, Danny Ozark—

"It isn't pollution that's harming the environment. It's the impurities in our air and water that are doing it." --Al Gore, Vice President—

"I love California. I practically grew up in Phoenix." --Dan Quayle—

"We've got to pause and ask ourselves: How much clean air do we need?" -- Lee Iacocca—

"The word 'genius' isn't applicable in football. A genius is a guy like Norman Einstein." --Joe Theisman—

"We don't necessarily discriminate. We simply exclude certain types of people." –Colonel Gerald Wellman, ROTC Instructor—

"If we don't succeed, we run the risk of failure." -- Bill Clinton, President—

"We are ready for an unforeseen event that may or may not occur." -- Al Gore, Vice President—

"Traditionally, most of Australia's imports come from overseas." – Keppel Enderbery—

"Your food stamps will be stopped effectively March 1992 because we received notice that you passed away. May God bless you. You may reapply if there is a change in your circumstances." --Department of Social Security Services, Greenville, South Carolina.

"If somebody has a bad heart, they can plug this jack in at night as they go to bed and it will monitor their heart throughout the night. And the next morning, when they wake up dead, there'll be a record." —Mark S. Fowler, FCC Chairman

KKK AT A SOUTHERN CHURCH

The Alabama preacher said to his Congregation, "Someone in this congregation has spread a rumor that I belong to the Ku Klux Klan. This is a horrible lie and one which a Christian community cannot tolerate. I am embarrassed and do not intend to accept this. Now, I want the party who did this to stand and ask forgiveness from God and this Christian family."

No one moved.

The preacher continued, "Do you have the nerve to face me and admit this is a falsehood? Remember, you will be forgiven and in your heart you will feel glory. Now stand and confess your transgression."

Again all was quiet.

Then slowly, a drop-dead gorgeous blonde with a body that would stop traffic rose from the third pew. Her head was bowed and her voice quivered as she spoke, "Reverend there has been a terrible misunderstanding, I never said you were a member of the Ku Klux Klan. I simply told a couple of my friends you were a wizard under the sheets."

ONE FOR THE LADIES

One day my housework-challenged husband decided to wash his sweatshirt. Seconds after he stepped into the laundry room, he shouted to me, "What setting do I use on the washing machine?"
"It depends," I replied. "What does it say on your shirt?"
He yelled back, "University of Iowa."
And they say blondes are dumb...

A couple is lying in bed. The man says, "I'm going to make you the happiest woman in the world." The woman replies, "I'll miss you..."

He said – Shall we try swapping positions tonight? She said – That's a good idea. You stand by the ironing board while I sit on the sofa and fart.

Q: What do you call an intelligent, good looking, sensitive man" A: A rumor.

A man and his wife, now in their 60's, were celebrating their 40th wedding anniversary. On their special day a good fairy came to them and said that because they had been so good that each one of them could have one wish. The wife wished for a trip around the world with her husband. Woosh! Immediately she had airline/cruise tickets in her hands. The man wished for a female companion 30 years younger... Whoosh, immediately he turned ninety!!! Gotta love that fairy!

Dear Lord, I pray for Wisdom to understand my man; Love to forgive him; And Patients for his moods. Because, Lord, if I pray for Strength, I'll beat him to death. AMEN.

Q: Why do little boys whine? A: They are practicing to be men.

Q: What do you call a handcuffed man? A: Trustworthy.

Q: What does it mean when a man is in your bed gasping for breath and calling your name? A: You did not hold the pillow down long enough.

Q: Why do men whistle when they are sitting on the toilet? A: It helps them remember which end they need to wipe.

Q: How do you keep your husband from reading your e-mail? A: Rename the mail folder "Instruction Manuals".

NEW ORLEANS SIGNS SEEN AFTER KATRINA

- Katrina gave me a Blow Job – I'll never forget.
- FEMA Evacuation Plan: Run Mother Fucker Run!

QUICKIES

Quickie #1
One day, Jay Dini came home and was greeted by his wife dressed in a very sexy nightie.
"Tie me up," she purred, "and you can do anything you want."
So he tied her and went fishing.

Quickie #2
A woman came home, screeching her car into the driveway, and ran into the house. She slammed the door and shouted at the tip of her lungs, "Honey, pack your bags, I won the lottery!"
The husband said, "Oh my gosh! What should I pack, beach stuff or mountain stuff?"
"Doesn't matter," she said. "Just get the hell out."

Quickie #3
Marriage is a relationship in which one person is always right, and the other is a husband.

Quickie #4
A Polish immigrant went to the DMV to apply for a driver's license. First, of course, he had to take an eye sight test. The optician showed him a card with the letters: C Z W I X N O S T A C Z.
"Can you read this?" the optician asked.
"Read it?" the Polish guy replied, "I know the guy!"

Quickie #5
Mother Superior called all the nuns together and said to them, "I must tell you all something. We have a case of gonorrhea in the convent."
"Thank goodness," said an elderly nun in the back. "I'm so tired of chardonnay."

Quickie #6

A wife was making a breakfast of fried eggs for her husband. Suddenly, her husband burst into the kitchen.

"Careful," he said, "Careful! Put in some more butter! Oh my gosh! You're cooking too many at once. TOO Many! Turn them! Turn them NOW!. We need more butter. Oh my gosh! Where are we going to get more butter? They're going to stick!

Careful...careful! I said be careful! You never listen to me when you're cooking! Never! Turn them! Turn them! Are you crazy? Have you lost your mind? Don't forget to salt them. You know you always forget to salt them. Use the salt. Use the salt! The salt! The salt!!!"

The wife stared at him. "What in the world is wrong with you" You think I don't know how to fry a couple eggs?"

The husband calmly replied, "I wanted to show you what it feels like when I'm driving."

Quickie #7

Fifty-one years ago, Herman James, a North Carolina mountain man, was drafted by the Army.

On his first day in basic training, the Army issued him a comb. That afternoon the Army barber sheared off all his hair.

On his second day, the Army issued Herman a toothbrush. That afternoon the dentist yanked seven of his teeth.

On the third day, the Army issued him a jock strap. The Army has been looking for Herman for 51 years!

JUSTICE SERVED

Remember the guy who got on a plane with a bomb built into his shoe and tried to light it? Did you know his trial is over? Did you know he was sentenced? Did you see/hear any of the judge's comments on TV or Radio? Didn't think so. Everyone should hear what the judge had to say.

Ruling by Judge William Young, US District Court.

Prior to sentencing, the Judge asked the defendant if he had anything to say. His response: After admitting his guilt to the court for the record, Reid also admitted his "allegiance to Osama bin Laden, to Islam, and to the religion of Allah," defiantly stating, "I think I will not apologize for my actions." And told the court "I am at war with your country."

Judge Young then delivered the following statement:

January 30, 2003, United States vs Reid. Judge Young:

"Mr. Richard C. Reid, hearken now the sentence the Court imposes upon you. On counts 1, 5 and 6 the Court sentences you to life in prison in the custody of the United States Attorney General. On counts 2, 3, 4 and 7, the Court sentences you to 20 years in prison on each count, the sentence on each count to run consecutively. (That's 80 years.)

On count 8 the Court sentences you to the mandatory 30 years again, to be served consecutively to the 80 years just imposed. The Court imposes upon you for each of the eight counts a fine of $250,000 that's an aggregate fine of $2 million. The Court accepts the government's recommendation with respect to restitution and orders restitution in the amount of $298.17 to Andre Bousquet and $5,784 to American Airlines.

The Court imposes upon you an $800 special assessment.

The Court imposes upon you five years supervised release simply because the law requires it. But the life sentences are real life sentences so I need go no further.
This is the sentence that is provided for by our statutes. It is a fair and just sentence. It is a righteous sentence.

Now, let me explain this to you. We are not afraid of you or any of your terrorist co-conspirators, Mr. Reid. We are Americans. We have been through the fire before. There is too much war talk here and I say that to every-one with the utmost respect. Here in this court, we deal with individuals as individuals and care for individuals as individuals. As human beings, we reach out for justice.

You are not an enemy combatant. You are a terrorist. You are not a soldier in any war. You are a terrorist. To give you that reference, to call you a soldier, gives you far too much stature. Whether the officers of government do it or your attorney does it, or if you think you are a soldier. You are not----you are a terrorist. And we do not negotiate with terrorist. We do not meet with terrorist. We do not sign documents with terrorists. We hunt them down one by one and bring them to justice.

So war talk is way out of line in this court. You are a big fellow. But you are not that big. You're no warrior. I've known warriors. You are a terrorist. A species of criminal that is guilty of multiple attempted murders. In a very real sense, State Trooper Santiago had it right when you first were taken off that plane and into custody and you wondered

93

where the press and the TV crews were, and he said: "You're no big deal."

You are no big deal!

What your able counsel and what the equally able United States attorneys have grappled with, is why you did something so horrific. What was it that led you here to this courtroom today?

I have listened respectfully to what you have to say. And I ask you to search your heart and ask yourself what sort of unfathomable hate led you to do what you are guilty and admit you are guilty of doing? And, I have an answer for you. It may not satisfy you, but as I search this entire record, it comes as close to understanding as I know.

It seems to me you hate the one thing that to us is most precious. You hate our freedom. Our individual freedom. Our individual freedom to live as we choose, to come and go as we choose, to believe or not believe as we individuals choose. Here, in this society, the very wind carries freedom. It carries it everywhere from sea to shining sea. It is because we prize individual freedom so much that you are here in this beautiful courtroom. So, that everyone can see, truly see, that justice is administered fairly, individually, and discretely. It is for freedom's sake that your lawyers are striving so vigorously on your behalf, have filed appeals, will go on in their representation of you before other judges.

We Americans are all about freedom. Because we all know that the way we treat you, Mr. Reid, is the measure of our own liberties. Make no mistake though. It is yet true that we will bear any burden; pay any price, to preserve our freedoms. Look around this courtroom. Mark it well. The world is not going to long remember what you or I say here. The day after tomorrow, it will be forgotten, but this, however, will long endure.

Here in this courtroom and courtrooms all across America, the American people will gather to see that justice, individual justice, justice, not war, individual justice is in fact being done. The very President of the United States through his officers will have to come into courtrooms and lay out evidence on which specific matters can be judged and juries of citizens will gather to sit and judge that evidence democratically, to mold shape and refine our sense of justice.

See that flag, Mr. Reid? That's the flag of the United States of America. That flag will fly long after this is all forgotten. That flag stands for freedom. And it always will.

Mr. Custody Officer. Stand him down.

YELLOW, PINK and GREEN

Mujibar was trying to get into the USA legally through immigration. The officer said, "Mujibar, you have passed all the tests, except there is one more test. Unless you pass it, you cannot enter the United States of America."

Mujibar said, "I am ready."

The officer said, "Make a sentence using the words yellow, pink and green."

Mujibar thought for a few minutes and said, "Mister Officer, I am ready."

The Officer said, "Go ahead."

Mujibar said, "The telephone goes green, green, green, and I pink it up, and say, 'yellow, this is Mujibar.'"

Mujibar now lives in a neighborhood near you and works at a credit card help desk. I talked to him yesterday.

STRANDED TOO LONG

One day this guy, who has been stranded on a desert island for ten years, sees an unusual speck on the horizon. As the speck gets closer and closer, he begins to rule out the possibilities of a small boat, even a raft. Suddenly, emerging from the surf comes this drop-dead gorgeous blonde woman in a wet suit and scuba gear. She approaches him and asks seductively, "How long has it been since you've had a cigarette?"

"Ten years!" he says. So she reaches over and unzips a waterproof pocket on her left sleeve and pulls out a fresh pack of cigarettes. He takes on, lights it, and after a long drag, says, "Man, oh man! Is that ever good!"

She then seductively inquires "How long has it been since you've had a sip of bourbon?" Trembling, he replies, "Ten Years!" So she reaches over and unzips a waterproof pocket on her right sleeve, then pulls out a flask, and gives it to him. He opens the flask, takes a long swig, and says, "Wow, that's absolutely fantastic!"

After this she starts to slowly undue the long zipper running down the front of her wet suit, pauses and looks at him seductively, "And how long has it been since you've played around?"

The poor guy, with tears in his eyes, replies, "Damn! Don't tell me you've got golf clubs in there."

ABBOT AND COSTELLO TODAY

If Bud Abbot and Lou Costello were alive today, their infamous sketch, "Who's on First?" might have turned out something like this:

Costello calls to buy a computer from Abbot.

Abbott: Super Duper computer store. Can I help you?
Costello: Thanks. I'm setting up an office in my den and I'm thinking about buying a computer.
Abbott: Mac?
Costello: No, the name's Lou.
Abbott: Your computer?
Costello: I don't own a computer. I want to buy one.
Abbott: Mac?
Costello: I told you, my name is Lou.
Abbott: What about Windows?
Costello: Why? Will it get stuffy in here?
Abbott: Do you want a computer with Windows?
Costello: I don't know. What will I see when I look at the windows?
Abbott: Wallpaper.
Costello: Never mind the windows. I need a computer and software.
Abbott: Software for Windows?
Costello: No. On the computer! I need something I can use to write proposals, track expenses and run my business. What do you have?
Abbott: Office.
Costello: Yeah, for my office. Can you recommend anything?
Abbott: I just did.
Costello: You just did what?
Abbott: Recommend something.
Costello: You recommended something?
Abbott: Yes.

Costello: For my office?

Abbott: Yes.

Costello: OK, what did you recommend for my office?

Abbott: Office.

Costello: Yes, for my office!

Abbott: I recommend Office and Windows.

Costello: I already have an office with windows! OK, let's just say I'm sitting at my computer and I want to type a proposal. What do I need?

Abbott: Word.

Costello: What word?

Abbott: Word in Office.

Costello: The only work in office is office.

Abbott: The Word in Office for Windows.

Costello: Which word in office for windows?

Abbott: The Word you get when you click the blue "W."

Costello: I'm going to clock your blue "w" if you don't start with some straight answers. What about financial bookkeeping? You have anything I can track my money with?

Abbott: Money.

Costello: That's right. What do you have?

Abbott: Money.

Costello: I need money to track my money.

Abbott: It comes bundled with your computer.

Costello: What's bundled with my computer?

Abbott: Money.

Costello: Money comes with my computer?

Abbott: Yes, No extra charge.

Costello. I get a bundle of money with my computer? How much?

Abbott: One copy.

Costello: Isn't it illegal to copy money?

Abbott: Microsoft gave us a license to copy Money.

Costello: They can give you a license to copy money?

Abbott: Why not? THEY OWN IT?

A few days later

Abbott: Super Duper computer store. Can I help you?
Costello: How do I turn my computer off?
Abbott: Click on "START"...

KIDS COMMERCIALS

A fifth grade teacher in a Christian school asked her class to look at TV commercials and see if they could use them in some way to communicate ides about God. Here are some of the results:

- God is like…Bayer Aspirin. He works miracles.
- God is like…a Ford. He's got a better idea.
- God is like…Coke. He's the real thing.
- God is like…Hallmark Cards. He cares enough to send His very best.
- God is like…Tide. He gets the stains out that others leave behind.
- God is like…Sears. He has everything.
- God is like…Alka-Seltzer. Try Him, you'll like Him.
- God is like…Scotch Tape. You can't see him, but you know He's there.
- God is like…Delta. He's ready when you are.
- God is like…Allstate. You're in good hands with Him.
- God is like…VO-5 Hair Spray. He holds through all kinds of weather.
- God is like…Dial Soap. Aren't you glad you have Him? Don't you wish everybody did?
- God is like…the U.S. Post Office. Neither rain, nor snow, nor sleet, nor ice will keep Him from His appointed destinations.

THE FLEA FLICKER

Two fleas from Detroit had an agreement to meet every winter in Miami for a vacation. Last year when one flea gets to Miami, he's all blue, shivering and shaking, darn near froze to death! The other flea asks him, "What the hell happened to you?"

The first flea says, "I rode down here in the mustache of a guy on a Harley."

The other flea responds saying, "That's the worst way to travel. Try what I do. Go to the Metro airport bar. Have a few drinks. While you are there, look for a nice stewardess. Crawl up her leg and nestle in where it's warm and cozy. It's the best way to travel that I can think of." The first flea thanks the second flea and says he will give it a try next winter.

A year goes by....When the first flea shows up in Miami he is all blue, and shivering and shaking again. Darn near froze to death. The second flea says, "Didn't you try what I told you?"

"Yes," says the first flea. "I did exactly as you said...I went to the Metro airport bar. I had a few drinks. Finally, this nice young stewardess came in. I crawled right up to her warm cozy spot. It was so nice and warm that I fell asleep immediately. When I woke up, I was back in the mustache of the guy on the Harley."

PHARMACOLOGY

In Pharmacology, all drugs have two names, a trade name and generic name. For example, the trade name of Tylenol also has a generic name of Acetaminophen. Aleve is also called Naproxen. Amoxil is also called Amoxicillin and Advil is also called Ibuprofen.

The FDA has been looking for a generic name for Viagra. After careful consideration by a team of government experts, it recently announced that it has settled on the generic name of Mydixarizin. Also considered were Mycoxafailin, Mydixadrupin, Mycoxafloppin, Dixafix, and of course, Ibepikin.

Pfizer Corp. announced today that Viagra will soon be available in liquid form, and will be marketed by Pepsi Cola as a power beverage suitable for use as a mixer. It will now be possible for a man to literally pour himself a stiff one. Obviously we can no longer call this a soft drink, and it gives new meaning to the names of "cocktails," "highballs" and just a good old-fashioned "stiff drink." Pepsi will market the new concoction by the name of: MOUNT & DO.

Thought for the day: There is more money being spent on breast implants and Viagra today than on Alzheimer's research. This means that by 2040, there should be a large elderly population with perky boobs and huge erections and absolutely no recollection of what to do with them.

OPEN THE BLINDS

The other day, my nine year old son wanted to know why we were at war…My husband looked at our son and then looked at me. My husband and I were in the Army during the Gulf War and we would be honored to serve and defend our Country again today. I knew that my husband would give him a good explanation.

My husband thought for a few minutes and then told my son to go stand in our front living room window. He said, Son, stand there and tell me what you see?

I see trees and cars and our neighbors' houses, he replied.

OK, now I want you to pretend that our house and our yard is the United States of America and you are President Bush.

Our son giggled and said OK.

Now son, I want you to look out the window and pretend that every house and yard on this block is a different country, my husband said.

OK Dad, I'm pretending.

Now I want you to stand there and look out the window and pretend you see Saddam come out of his house with his wife, he has her by the hair and is hitting her. You see her bleeding and crying. He hits her in the face, he throws her on the ground, then he starts to kick her to death. Their children run out and are afraid to stop him, they are screaming and crying, they are watching this but do nothing because they are kids and they are afraid of their father. You see all of this, son…what do you do?

Dad? cried our son.

What do you do son?

I'd call the police, Dad.

OK, Pretend that the police are the United Nations. They take your call. They listen to what you know and saw, but they refuse to help. What do you do then, son?

Dad…but the police are supposed to help! My son starts to whine.

They don't want to son, because they say that it is not their place or your place to get involved and that you should stay out of it, my husband says.

But Dad…he killed her, my son exclaims.

I know he did…but the police tell you to stay out of it. Now I want you to look out that window and pretend you see our neighbor who you're pretending is Saddam turn around and do the same thing to his children.

Daddy…he kills them?

Yes son, he does. What do you do?

Well, if the police don't want to help, I will go and ask my next door neighbor to help me stop him, our son says.

Son, our next door neighbor sees what is happening and refuses to get involved as well. He refuses to open the door and help you stop him, my husband says.

But Dad, I NEED help! I can't stop him by myself!

What do you do son?

Our son starts to cry.

OK, no one wants to help you, the man across the street saw you ask for help and saw that no one would help you stop him. He stands taller and puffs out his chest. Guess what he does next son?

What Daddy?

He walks across the street to the old ladies house and breaks down her door and drags her out, steals all her stuff and sets her house on fire and then...he kills her. He turns around and sees you standing in the window and laughs at you. What do you do?

Daddy...

What do you do?

Our son is crying and he looks down and he whispers, I'd close the blinds, Daddy.

My husband looks at our son with tears in his eyes and asks him: why?

Because Daddy...the police are supposed to help people who need them...and they won't help... You always say that neighbors are supposed to HELP neighbors, but they won't help either...they won't help me stop him...I'm afraid...I can't do it by myself daddy...I can't look out my window and just watch him do all these terrible things and...and...do nothing...so...I'm going to close the blinds...so I can't see what he's doing...and I'm going to pretend that it is not happening.

I start to cry. My husband looks at our nine year old son standing in the window, looking pitiful and ashamed at his answers to my husband's questions and he says…Son.

Yes, Daddy.

Open the blinds because that man…he's at your front door…What do you do?

My son looks at his father, anger and defiance in his eyes. He balls up his tiny fists and looks his father square in the eyes, without hesitation he says: I defend my family, Dad! I'm not gonna let him hurt Mommy or my sister, Dad! I'm gonna fight him!!!

I see a tear rolls down my husband's cheek and he grabs our son to his chest and hugs him tight, and says… It's too late to fight him, he's too strong and he's already at your front door, son…you should have stopped him before he killed his wife, and his children and the old lady across the way. You have to do what's right, even if you have to do it alone, before it's too late, my husband whispers.

That scenario I just gave you is why we are at war with Iraq. When good men stand by and let evil happen, soon the greatest atrocities in the world won't affect them.

You must never ever be afraid to do what is right! Even if you have to do it alone! Be proud to be an American! Be proud of our troops! Support them! Support America so that in the future our children will never have to close their blinds.

NO PASSPORT

An elderly Canadian gentleman of 83 arrived in Paris by plane. At the French customs desk, the man took a few minutes to locate his passport in his carry-on bag.

"Have you been to France before, monsieur?" the customs officer asked, sarcastically. The elderly gentleman admitted he had been to France previously. "Then you should know enough to have your passport ready."

The Canadian said, "The last time I was here, I didn't have to show it."

"Impossible, Canadians always have to show their passports on arrival in France!"

The Canadian senior gave the Frenchman a long hard look, then he quietly explained, "Well, when I came ashore at Juno Beach on D-Day in 1944 to help liberate this country, I couldn't find any Frenchman to show it to."

COMPUTERS AND CARS

For all of us who feel only the deepest love and affection for the way computers have enhanced our lives, please read on. At a recent computer expo (COMDEX), Bill Gates reportedly compared the computer industry with the auto industry and stated, "If GM had kept up with technology like the computer industry has, we would all be driving $25.00 cars that get 1,000 miles to the gallon."

In response to Bill's comments, GM issued a press release stating: If GM had developed technology like Microsoft, we would all be driving cars with the following characteristics:

1. For no reason whatsoever, your car would crash twice a day.

2. Every time they repainted the lines in the road, you would have to buy a new car.

3. Occasionally your car would die on the freeway for no reason. You would have to pull to the side of the road, close all of the windows. Shut off the car, restart it, and reopen all the windows before you could continue. For some reason you would simply accept this.

4. Occasionally, executing a maneuver such as a left turn would cause your car to shut down and refuse to restart, in which case you would have to reinstall the engine.

5. Macintosh would make a car that was powered by the sun, was reliable, five times as fast and twice as easy to drive – but would run on only five percent of the roads.

6. The oil, water temperature, and alternator warning lights would all be replaced by a single "This Car Has Performed an Illegal Operation" warning light.

7. The airbag system would ask, "Are you sure?" before deploying.

8. Occasionally, for no reason whatsoever, your car would lock you out and refuse to let you in until you simultaneously lifted the door handle, turned the key and grabbed hold of the radio antenna.

9. Every time a new car was introduced, car buyers would have to learn how to drive all over again because none of the controls would operate in the same manner as the old car.

10. You'd have to press the "Start" button to turn the engine off.

MEN, MEN, MEN!!!

1. How many men does it take to open a beer? None. It should be opened when she brings it.

2. Why is a Laundromat a really bad place to pick up a woman? Because a woman who can't even afford a washing machine will probably never be able to support you.

3. Why do women have smaller feet than men? It's one of those "evolutionary things" that allows them to stand closer to the kitchen sink.

4. How do you know when a woman is about to say something smart? When she starts a sentence with "A man once told me…"

5. How do you fix a woman's watch? You don't. There is a clock on the oven.

6. Why do men fart more than women? Because women can't shut up long enough to build up the required pressure.

7. If your dog is barking at the back door and your wife is yelling at the front door, who do you let in first? The dog, of course. He'll shut up once you let him in.

8. What's the worse than a Male Chauvinist Pig? A woman who won't do what she's told.

9. I married a Miss Right. I just didn't know her first name was Always.

10. Scientists have discovered a food that diminishes a woman's sex drive by 90%. It's called a Wedding Cake.

11. Why do men die before their wives? They want to.

12. Women will never be equal to men until they can walk down the street with a bald head and a beer gut, and still think they are sexy.

13. In the beginning, God created the earth and rested. Then God created Man and rested. Then God created Women. Since then, neither God nor Man has rested.

GO FLY A KITE

A husband in his back yard is trying to fly a kite. He throws the kite up in the air, the wind catches it for a few seconds, then it comes crashing back down to earth. He tries this a few more times with no success.

All the while, his wife is watching from the kitchen window, muttering to herself how men need to be told how to do everything. She opens the window and yells to her husband, "You need a piece of tail."

The man turns with a confused look on his face and says, "Make up your mind. Last night, you told me to go fly a kite."

SMILES

- Now that food has replaced sex in my life, I can't even get into my own pants.

- Marriage changes passion. Suddenly you're in bed with a relative.

- I saw a woman wearing a sweat shirt with "Guess" on it. So I said "Implants?" She hit me.

- How come we choose from just two people to run for President and over fifty for Miss America?

- A good friend will come and bail you out of jail…but, a true friend will be sitting next to you saying, "Wow…that was fun!"

- I signed up for an exercise class and was told to wear loose-fitting clothing. If I had any loose-fitting clothing, I wouldn't have signed up in the first place!

- When I was young we used to go "skinny dipping." Now I just "chunky dunk."

- Don't argue with an idiot; people watching may not be able to tell the difference.

- Wouldn't it be nice if whenever we messed up our life we could simply press 'Ctrl Alt Delete' and start all over. Amen, Amen!!

- Why is it that our children can't read a Bible in school, but they can in prison?

- Wouldn't you know it.... Brain cells come and brain cells go, but FAT cells live forever

- Why do I have to swear on the Bible in court when the Ten Commandments cannot be displayed outside?

- Bumper sticker of the year: "If you can read this, thank a teacher – and, since it's in English, thank a soldier."

- And remember: life is like a roll of toilet paper. The closer it gets to the end, the faster it goes.

SEVEN DWARFS GO TO THE VATICAN

The seven dwarfs go to the Vatican, and because they are THE seven dwarfs, they are ushered in to see the Pope.

Dopey leads the pack. "Dope, my son," says the Pope. "What can I do for you?" Dopey asks, "Excuse me your Excellence, but are there any dwarf nuns in Rome?" The Pope wrinkles his brow at the odd question, thinks for a moment and answers, "No, Dopey, there are no dwarf nuns in Rome."

In the background a few of the dwarfs start giggling. Dopey turns around and gives them a glare, silencing them. Dopey turns back, "Your Worship, are there any dwarf nuns in all of Europe?" The Pope, puzzled now, again thinks for a moment and then answers, "No, Dopey, there are no dwarf nuns in Europe."

This time, all of the other dwarfs burst into laughter. Once again, Dopey turns around and silences them, with an angry glare. Dopey turns back and says, "Mr. Pope! Are there ANY dwarf nuns anywhere in the world?"

"I'm sorry, my son, there are no dwarf nuns anywhere in the world."

The other dwarfs collapse into a heap, rolling and laughing, pounding the floor, tears rolling down their cheeks, as they begin chanting... "Dopey screwed a penguin...Dopey screwed a penguin!"

SCOOBY DOOBY DOODY

A flat-chested young lady went to Dr. Smith for advice about enlarging her breasts. He told her, "Every day when you get out of the shower, rub your nipples and say, Scooby Doobie Doobies, I want bigger boobies."

So she did this faithfully for several months, and it worked! She grew great boobs!

One morning she was running late and when she was on the bus she realized she had forgotten her morning ritual. At this point she loved her new boobs and didn't want to lose them. So she got up, right in the middle of the bus, and said, "Scooby Doobie Doobie, I want bigger boobies."

The guy sitting nearby asked her, "Do you go to Dr. Smith by any chance?"

"Why yes, I do. How did you know?"

He leaned toward her and whispered, "Hickory dickory dock,"

THE BILL OF NON-RIGHTS

"We the sensible people of the Unites States, in an attempt to help everyone get along, restore some semblance of justice, avoid more riots, keep our nation safe, promote positive behavior, and secure the blessings of debt free liberty to ourselves and our great-great-great-grandchildren, hereby try one more time to ordain and establish some common sense guidelines for the terminally whiny, guilt ridden, and delusional. We hold these truths to be self-evident: that a whole lot of people are confused by the Bill of Rights and are so dim they require Bill of NON-Rights."

ARTICLE I: You do not have the right to a new car, big screen TV, or any other form of wealth. More power to you if you can legally acquire them, but no one is guaranteeing anything.

ARTICLE II: You do not have the right to never be offended. This country is based on freedom, and that means freedom for everyone – not just you! You may leave the room, turn the channel, express a different opinion, etc.; but the world is full of idiots, and probably always will be.

ARTICLE III: You do not have the right to be free from harm. If you stick a screwdriver in your eye, learn to be more careful; do not expect the tool manufacturer to make you and all your relatives independently wealthy.

ARTICLE IV: You do not have the right to free food and housing. Americans are the most charitable people to be found and will gladly help anyone in need, but we are quickly growing weary of subsidizing generation after generation of professional couch potatoes who achieve nothing more than the creation of another generation of professional couch potatoes.

ARTICLE V: You do not have the right to free health care. That would be nice, but from the looks of public housing, we're just not interested in public health care.

ARTICLE VI: You do not have the right to physically harm other people. If you kidnap, rape, intentionally maim, or kill someone, don't be surprised if the rest of us want to see you fry in the electric chair.

ARTICLE VII: You do not have the right to the possessions of others. If you rob, cheat, or coerce away the goods or services of other citizens, don't be surprised if the rest of us get together and lock you away in a place where you still won't have the right to a big screen color TV or a life of leisure.

ARTICLE VIII: You do not have the right to a job. All of us sure want you to have a job, and will gladly help you along in hard times, but we expect you to take advantage of the opportunities of education and vocational training laid before you to make yourself useful.

ARTICLE IX: You do not have the right to happiness. Being an American means that you have the right to PURSUE happiness which, by the way, is a lot easier if you are unencumbered by an overabundance of idiotic laws created by those of you who were confused by the Bill of Rights.

ARTICLE X: This is an English speaking country. We don't care where you are from, English is our language. Learn it or go back to wherever you come from!

ARTICLE XI: You do not have the right to change our country's history or heritage. This country was founded on the belief in one true GOD. And yet, you are given the freedom to believe in any religion, any faith, or no faith at all; with no fear of persecution. The phrase IN GOT WE TRUST is part of our heritage and history and if you are uncomfortable with in, TOUGH!!!!

If you agree, you <u>are invited</u> to share this with a friend. No, you don't have to, and nothing tragic will befall you if you don't. I just think it's about time common sense is allowed to flourish.

- Sensible people of the United States speak out, because if you don't, stupid people will.

SENIORS

Let's hear it for the seniors.

A very self-important college freshman at a recent football game, toot it upon himself to explain to a senior citizen sitting next to him why it was impossible for the older generation to understand his own. "You grew up in a different, actually almost primitive world," the student said loud enough for the whole crowd to hear. "We young people today grew up with television, jet planes, space travel, man walking on the moon, our spaceships have visited Mars.... We even have nuclear energy, electric and hydrogen cars, computers with light-speed processing...and uh...."

Taking advantage of the pause for breath in the student's litany, the "wizened" one said, "You're right, son. We didn't have those things when we were young.... So... we invented them...you arrogant little shithead!! Now...what are you doing for the next generation??"

INDIAN CHIEF

An old Indian Chief sat in his hut on the reservation, smoking a ceremonial pipe and eyeing two US government officials sent to interview him.

One US Official asked Chief Two Eagles, "You have observed the white man for 90 years. You've seen his wars and his technological advances. You've seen his progress, and the damage he's done."

The Chief nodded in agreement. The official continued, "Considering all these events, in your opinion, where did the white man go wrong?"

The Chief stared at the government officials for over a minute and then calmly replied, "When white man found the land, Indians were running it. No taxes, no debt, plenty buffalo, plenty beaver, women did all the work, medicine man free, Indian man spent all day hunting and fishing, all night having sex."

Then the Chief leaned back and smiled. "Only white man dumb enough to think he could improve system like that."

AMERICAN JOBS

Joe Smith started the day early having set his alarm clock (made in Japan) for 6am. While his coffeepot (made in China) was perking, he shaved with his electric razor (made in Hong Kong). He put on a dress shirt (made in Sri Lanka), designer jeans (made in Singapore) and tennis shoes (made in Korea). After cooking his breakfast in his new electric skillet (made in India) he sat down with his calculator (made in Mexico) to see how much he could spend today. After setting his watch (made in Taiwan) to the radio (made in India) he got in his car (made in Germany) filled it gas from Saudi Arabia and continued his search for a good paying AMERICAN JOB. At the end of yet another discouraging and fruitless day checking his computer (made in Malaysia), Joe decided to relax for a while. He put on his sandals (made in Brazil), poured himself a glass of wine (made in France) and turned on his TV (made in Indonesia), and then wondered why he can't find a good paying job in AMERICA.

HERE'S YOUR SIGN

Stupid people should have to wear signs that just say, "I'm Stupid." That way you wouldn't rely on them, would you? You wouldn't ask them anything. It would be like, "Excuse me…oops…never mind, didn't see your sign."

It's like before my wife and I moved. Our house was full of boxes and there was a U-Haul truck in our driveway. My neighbor comes over and says, "Hey, you moving?"

"Nope. We just pack our stuff up once or twice a month to see how many boxes it takes. Here's your sign."

A couple of months ago I went fishing with a buddy of mine, we pulled his boat into the dock, I lifted up this big ol' stringer of bass and this idiot on the dock goes, "Hey, y'all catch all them fish?"

"Nope. Talked 'em into giving up. Here's your sign."

I was watching one of those animal shows on the Discovery Channel. There was a guy inventing a shark bite suit. And there's only one way to test it.

"Alright, Jimmy, you got that shark suit on, it looks good…. They want you to jump into this pool of sharks, and you tell us if it hurts when they bite you."

"Well, all right, but hold my sign. I don't wanna lose it."

Last time I had a flat tire, I pulled my truck into one of those side-of-the-road gas stations. The attendant walks out, looks at my truck, looks at me, and I swear he said, "Tire go flat?"

I couldn't resist. I said, "Nope. I was driving around and those other three just swelled right up on me. Here's your sign."

We were trying to sell our car about a year ago. A guy came over to the house and drove the car around for about 45 minutes. We get back to the house, he gets out of the car, reaches down and grabs the exhaust pipe, then says, "Damn that's hot!" See, if he'd been wearing his sign, I could have stopped him.

I learned to drive an 18-wheeler in my days of adventure. Wouldn't you know, I misjudged the height of a bridge. The truck got stuck and I couldn't get it out, no matter how I tried. I radioed in for help and eventually a local cop shows up to take the report. He went through his basic questioning…okay…no problem. I thought for sure he was clear of needing a sign…until he asked, "So, is your truck stuck?"

I couldn't help myself! I looked at him, looked back at the rig and then back to him and said, "No, I'm delivering a bridge…here's your sign."

I stayed late at work one night and a co-worker looked at me and said, "Are you still here?"

I replied, "No. I left about 10 minutes ago. Here's your sign."

MORE HILLBILLIES

Bubba and Junior were standing at the base of the flagpole, looking up. A blond lady walked by and asked what they were doing. We're supposed to find the height of the flagpole," said Bubba, "but we don't have a ladder."

The woman took a wrench from her purse, loosened a few bolts, and laid the pole down. Then she took a tape measure from her pocket, took a measurement and announced, "Eighteen feet, six inches," and walked away.

Junior shook his head and laughed. "Ain't that just like a dumb blond? We ask for the height, and she gives us the length."

BRAVE MEN JOKES

Man walks into the bedroom with a sheep under his arm while his wife is lying in bed reading. Man says: "this is the pig I have sex with when you've got a headache." Wife replies: "I think you'll find, that you have a sheep." Man replies: "I think you'll find I was talking to the sheep."

A man walks into his bedroom and sees his wife packing a suitcase. He asks, "What are you doing?" She answers, "I'm moving to Sydney. I hear prostitutes there get paid $400 for doing what I do for you for free." Later that night, on her way out, the wife walks into the bedroom and sees her husband packing his suitcase. When she asks him where he's going, he replies, "I'm coming too, I want to see how you live on $800 a year."

A woman was shopping at her local supermarket where she selected:
- 2 liters of low fat milk.

- A carton of eggs.

- 2 liters of orange juice.

- A head of lettuce.

- Half dozen tomatoes.

- A 500g jar of coffee.

- A 250g pack of bacon.

As she was unloading her items on the conveyor belt to check out, a drunk standing behind her watched as she placed the items in front of the cashier. While the cashier was ringing up her purchases, the drunk calmly stated, "You must be single." The woman was a bit startled by this proclamation, but she was intrigued by the derelict's intuition, since she was indeed single. She looked at her six items on the belt and saw nothing particularly unusual about her selections that could have tipped off the drunk to her material status.

Curiosity getting the better of her, she said, "Well, you know what, you're absolutely correct. But how on earth did you know that?" The drunk replied, "Cause you're ugly."

PRODUCT ENDORSEMENTS

I am writing to say what an excellent product you have. I've used it all of my married life, as my mom always told me it was the best. Now that I am in my fifties I find it even better. In fact, about a month ago, I spilled some red wine on my new white blouse.

My inconsiderate and uncaring husband started to belittle me about how clumsy I was and generally started becoming a pain in the neck. One thing led to another and somehow I ended up with his blood on my new white blouse!

I grabbed my bottle of Tide with bleach alternative and to my surprise and satisfaction, all of the stains came out. In fact, the stains came out so well the detectives who came by yesterday told me that the DNA tests on my blouse were negative and then my attorney called and said that I was no longer considered a suspect in the disappearance of my husband.

What a relief! Going through menopause is bad enough without being a murder suspect. I thank you, once again, for having a great product. Well, gotta go, have to write to the Hefty bag people.

GOOD COMMUNICATION IS THE KEY

A pastor wanted to raise money for his church and, on being told there was a fortune in horse racing, decided to buy one and enter it in the races. However, at the local auction, the going price for a horse was so high that he ended up buying a donkey instead.

He thought that since he had it he might as well go ahead and entered it in the race and, much to his surprise, the donkey came in third. The next day the local paper carried this headline:
    ** PASTOR'S ASS SHOWS**

The pastor was so pleased with the donkey that he entered it in another race and this time it won. The local paper read:
    ** PASTOR'S ASS OUT FRONT**

The Bishop was so upset with this kind of publicity that he ordered the pastor not to enter the donkey in another race. The next day, the local paper headline read:
    BISHOP SCRATCHES PASTOR'S ASS

This was too much for the Bishop, so he ordered the pastor to get rid of the donkey. The pastor decided to give it to a nun in a nearby convent. The local paper, hearing of the news, posted the following headline the next day:
    NUN HAS BEST ASS IN TOWN

The Bishop fainted. He informed the nun that she would have to get rid of the donkey, so she sold it to a farmer for ten dollars. The next day, the paper read:
    ** Nun sells ass for $10 **

This was too much for the Bishop, so he ordered the nun to buy back the donkey and lead it to the plains where it could run wild. Headlines read:

** NUN ANNOUNCES HER ASS IS WILD AND FREE **

The Bishop was buried the next day.

HI TED

After numerous rounds of "We don't know if he is still alive," Osama himself decided to send Ted Kennedy a letter in his own handwriting to let him know he was still in the game.

Kennedy opened the letter which appeared to contain a single line of coded message:

370HSSV - 0773H

Kennedy was baffled, so he e-mailed it to John Kerry. Kerry and his aides had no clue either, so they sent it to the FBI. No one could solve it at the FBI, so it went to the CIA, then to the NSA.

With no clue as to its meaning, the NSA finally asked The Marine Corps Intelligence division for help. Within a few seconds the Marines cabled back with this reply: "Tell Kennedy he's holding the message upside down."

RICHARD SIMMON'S
LATEST WEIGHT LOSS PROGRAM

A guy calls a company and orders their 5-day, 10 lb. weight loss program.

The next day, there's a knock on the door and there dressed in nothing but a pair of Nike running shoes, a tiny Bikini and a sign around her neck is a beautiful girl. She introduces herself as a representative of the weight loss company.

The sign reads: "If you can catch me, you have me." Without a second thought, he takes off after her. A few miles later, huffing and puffing, he finally catches her and gets his reward.

The same girl shows up for the next four days and the same thing happens. On the fifth day, he weighs himself and is delighted to find he has lost 10 lbs. as promised. He then calls the company and orders their 5-day 20 lb program.

The next day there's a knock at the door and there stands the most stunning, beautiful, sexy woman he has ever seen in his life. She is wearing nothing but Reebok running shoes, an even smaller bikini that the first girl and a sign around her neck that reads: "If you catch me you can have me."

Well, he's out the door after her like a shot! This girl is in excellent shape and it takes him a while to catch her; but when he does, it's definitely worth every muscle cramp and wheeze, so for the next four days, the same routine happens.

Much to his delight, on the fifth day he weighs himself only to discover that he has lost another 20 lbs. as promised. He decides to go for broke and calls the company to order the 7-day 50 pound program.

"Are you sure?" asks the representative on the phone. "This is our most rigorous program."

"Absolutely," he replies, "I haven't felt this good in years."

The next day there's a knock at the door; and when he opens it he finds this huge, muscular, 7 foot man standing there, wearing nothing but a tiny speedo, pink running shoes and a sign around his neck that reads: "I'm Bart. If I catch you, you're mine...."

TRIPS TO WALMART
WILL NEVER BE THE SAME

Dear Mrs. Fenton,

Over the past six months, your husband, Mr. Bill Fenton has been causing quite a commotion in our store. We cannot tolerate this type of behavior and have considered banning the entire family from shopping in any of our stores.

We have documented all incidents on our video surveillance equipment. Three of our clerks are attending counseling from the trouble your husband has caused. All complaints against Mr. Fenton have been compiled and are listed below.

Mr. Wally Worrywart
President
WalMart Complaint Department

MEMO

Re: Mr. Bill Fenton – Complaints – 15 Things Mr. Bill Fenton has done while his spouse/partner is shopping:

1. June 15, took 24 boxes of condoms and randomly put them in people's carts when they weren't looking.
2. July 2, set all the alarm clocks in housewares to go off at 5-minute intervals.
3. July 7, made a trail of tomato juice on the floor leading to the rest rooms.

4. July 19, walked up to an employee and told her in an official tone, "Code 3 in Housewares…"and watched what happened.

5. August 4, went to the Service Desk and asked to put a bag of M&M's on lay away.

6. September 14, moved a "CAUTION – WET FLOOR" sign to a carpeted area.

7. September 15, Set up a tent in the camping department and told other shoppers he'd invite them in if they'll bring pillows from the bedding department.

8. September 23, When a clerk asks if they can help him, he begins to cry and asks, "Why can't you people just leave me alone?"

9. October 4, Looked right into the security camera; used it as a mirror, and picked his nose.

10. November 10, While handling guns in the hunting department, asked the clerk if he knows where the antidepressants are.

11. December 3, Darted around the store suspiciously loudly humming the "Mission Impossible" theme.

12. December 6, In the auto department, practiced his "Madonna look" using different size funnels.

13. December 18, Hid in a clothing rack and when people browsed through, yelled "Pick me! Pick me!"

14. December 21, When an announcement came over the loud speaker, he assumes the fetal position and screams "No! No! It's those voices again!!!!

15. December 23, Went into a fitting room, shut the door and waited a while; then, yelled, very loudly, "There is no toilet paper in here!"

2007

CUP OF TEA

One day my mother was out and my dad was in charge of me. I was 2 maybe 2½ years old and had just recovered from an accident.

Someone had given me a little 'tea set' as a get-well gift and it was one of my favorite toys.

Daddy was in the living room engrossed in the evening news when I brought Daddy a little cup of 'tea,' which was just water. After several cups of tea and lots of praise for such yummy tea, my Mom came home.

My Dad made her wait in the living room to watch me bring him a cup of tea. Because it was 'just the cutest thing!' My Mom waited, and sure enough, here I come down the hall with a cup of tea for Daddy and she watches him drink it up.

Then she says, (as only a mother would know…:)

"Did it ever occur to you that the only place that baby can reach to get water is the toilet?"

LITTLE TYRONE IS AT IT AGAIN

- A new teacher was trying to make use of her psychology courses. She started her class by saying, "Everyone who thinks they're stupid, stand up!" After a few seconds, Little Tyrone stood up. The teacher said, "Do you think you're stupid, Little Tyrone?" "No, ma'am, but I hate to see you standing there all by yourself!"

- Little Tyrone watched, fascinated, as his mother smoothed cold cream on her face. "Why do you do that, mommy?" he asked. "To make myself beautiful," said his mother, who then began removing the cream with a tissue. "What's the matter?" asked Little Tyrone. "Giving up?"

- The math teacher saw that Little Tyrone wasn't paying attention in class. She called on him and said, "Tyrone! What are 2 and 4 and 28 and 44?" Little Tyrone quickly replied, "NBC, FOX, ESPN and the Cartoon Network!"

- Little Tyrone's kindergarten class was on a field trip to their local police station where they saw pictures tacked to a bulletin board of the 10 most wanted criminals. One of the youngsters pointed to a picture and asked if it really was the photo of a wanted person. "Yes," said the policeman. "The detectives want very badly to capture him." Little Tyrone asked, "Why didn't you keep him when you took his picture?"

- Little Tyrone attended a horse auction with his father. He watched as his father moved from horse to horse, running his hands up and down the horse's legs and rump. After a few minutes, Tyrone asked, "Dad, why are you doing that?" His father replied, "Because when I'm buying horses, I have to make sure that they are healthy and in good shape before I

138

buy." Tyrone looked worried, said, "Dad, I think the UPS guy wants to buy Mom."

Too often, we lose sight of life's simple pleasures. Remember, when someone annoys you it takes 42 muscles in your face to frown, BUT, it only takes 4 muscles to extend your arm and bitch-slap that mother&@)$?* upside the head!

THE ITALIAN ELBOW

An Italian grandmother is giving directions to her grown grandson who is coming to visit with his wife.

"You comma to de front door of the apartmenta. I am inna apartmenta 301. There issa bigga panel at the front door. With your elbow, pucha button 301. I will buzza you in. Come inside, the elevator is on the right. Get in, and with you elbow, puccha 3. When you get out, I'mma on the left. With you elbow, hit my doorbell."

"Grandma, that sounds easy, but, why am I hitting all these buttons with my elbow?"

"What…? You comma empty handed?"

WHO IS JACK SCHITT

For some time many of us have wondered just who is Jack Schitt? We find ourselves at a loss when someone says, "You don't know Jack Schitt!"

Well, thanks to my genealogy efforts, you can now respond in an intellectual way.

Jack Schitt is the only son of Awe Schitt. Awe Schitt, the fertilizer magnate, married O. Schitt, the owner of Needeep N. Schitt, Inc. They had one son, Jack.

Jack Schitt married Noe Schitt. The deep religious couple produced six children: Holie Schitt, Giva Schitt, Fulla Schitt, Bull Schitt, and the twins Deepp Schitt and Dip Schitt.

Against her parents' objections, Deep Schitt married Dumb Schitt, a high-school dropout. After being married 15 years, Jack and Noe Schitt divorced. Noe Schitt later married Ted Sherlock, and because her kids were living with them, she wanted to keep her previous name. She was known as Noe Schitt Sherlock.

Meanwhile, Dip Schitt married Loda Schitt, and they produced a son with a rather nervous disposition named Chicken Schitt. Two of the other six children, Fulla Schitt and Giva Schitt were inseparable throughout childhood and subsequently married the Happens brothers in a dual ceremony. The wedding announcement in the newspaper announced the Schitt-Happens nuptials. The Schitt-Happens children were Dawg, Byrd and Horse.

Bull Schitt, the prodigal son, left home to tour the world. He recently returned from Italy with his new Italian bride, Pisa Schitt.

Now when someone says, "You don't know Jack Schitt," you can correct them.

Sincerely,
Crock O. Schitt

10 RULES FOR
THANKSGIVING DINNER AT MY HOUSE

1. Don't get in line asking questions about the food. "Who made the potato salad? Is it egg in there? Are the greens fresh? Is the meat in the greens turkey or pork? Who made the macaroni and cheese? What kind of pie is that? Who made it? Ask one more question and I will punch you in your mouth, knocking out all your fronts so you won't be able to eat anything.

2. If you can't walk or are missing any limbs, sit your ass down until someone makes your plate for you. Dinner time is not the time for you to be independent. Nibble on them damn pecans and walnuts to hold you over until someone makes you a plate.

3. If you have kids under the age of twelve, I will escort their little asses to the basement and bring their food down to them. They are not gonna tear my damn house. Tell them that they are not allowed upstairs until it's time for Uncle Butchie to start telling family stories about their mommas and papas. If they come upstairs for any reason except for that they are bleeding to death, I will break a foot off in their ass!

4. There is going to be one prayer for Thanksgiving dinner! JUST ONE! We do not care that you are thankful that your 13 year old daughter gave birth to a healthy baby or your nephew just got out of jail. Save that talk for somebody who gives a damn. The time limit for the prayer is one minute. If you are still talking after that one minute is up, you will feel something hard come across your lips and they will be swollen for approximately 20 minutes.

5. Finish everything on your plate before you go up for seconds! If you don't, you will be cursed out and asked to stay your greedy ass home next year!

6. Bring your own Tupperware!! Don't let me catch you fixing yourself a plate in my good Tupperware knowing damn will that I will never see it again! Furthermore, if you didn't bring anything over, don't let me catching you making a plate period or it will be a misunderstanding.

7. What you came with is what you should leave with!! Do not leave my house with anything that doesn't belong to you. Everybody will be subject to a body search coming and going out of my domain.

8. Do not leave your kids so you can go hopping form house to house. This is not a daycare center. There will be a kid-parent roll call every ten minutes. Any parent that is not present at the time of roll call, your child will be put outside until you come and get him or her. After 24 hours, I will call DHS on your ignorant ass.

9. Book your hotel room before you come into town. There will be no sleeping over at my house. You are to come and eat dinner and take your ass home or to your hotel room. Everybody gets kick the hell out at 11:00 PM. You will get a 15 minute warning bell ring.

10. Last but not least. One plate per person. This is not a soup kitchen. I am not trying to feed your family until Christmas dinner. You will be surprised when you fix your plate. Anything over the appropriate amount will be charged to you before you leave. There will be a cash register at the door. Thanks to Cousin Alfred and his greed ass family, we now have a credit card machine. So Visa and MasterCard are now being accepted. No food stamps or access cards yet.

REDNECK MAMA

A woman walks into the downtown welfare office, trailed by 15 kids. "Wow," the social worker exclaims, "are they all yours???"

"Yep they are all mine." The flustered momma sighs, having heard that question a thousand times before. She says, "Sit down Leroy." All the children rush to find seats.

"Well," says the social worker, "then you must be here to sign up. I'll need all your children's names."

"This one's my oldest – he is Leroy." "OK, and who's next?" "Well, this one he is Leroy also."

The social worker raises an eyebrow but continues. One by one, through the oldest four, all boys, all named Leroy. Then she is introduced to the eldest girl, named Leighroy! "All right," says the caseworker. "I'm seeing a pattern here. Are they all named Leroy?"

Their Momma replied, "Well, yes – it makes it easier. When it is time to get them out of bed and ready for school, I yell, 'Leroy!' An' when it's time for dinner, I just yell 'Leroy,' an' they all comes arunnin.

"An' if I need to stop the kid who's running into the street, I just yell 'Leroy!' an' all of them stop. It's the smartest idea I ever had, namin' them all Leroy."

The social worker thinks this over for a bit, then wrinkles her forehead and says tentatively, "But what if you just want one kid to come, and not the whole bunch?"

"I call them by their last names."

GEORGE CARLIN

What a difference a sad event in someone's life makes. George Carlin's wife recently died. Isn't it amazing that George, a comedian of the 70's and 80's – could write something so very eloquent…and so very appropriate?

The paradox of our time in history is that we have taller buildings, but shorter tempers, wider freeways, but narrower viewpoints. We spend more, but have less, we buy more, but enjoy less. We have bigger houses and smaller families, more conveniences, but less time. We have more degrees, but less sense, more knowledge, but less judgment, more experts, and yet more problems, more medicine, but less wellness.

We drink too much, smoke too much, spend too recklessly, laugh too little, drive too fast, get too angry, stay up too late, get too tired, read too little, watch TV too much, and pray too seldom.

We have multiplied our possessions, but reduced our values. We talk too much, love too seldom, and hate too often.

We've learned how to make a living, but not a life. We've added years to life not life to years. We've been all the way to the moon and back, but have trouble crossing the street to meet a new neighbor. We conquered outer space, but not inner space. We've done larger things, but not better things.

We've cleaned up the air, but polluted the soul. We've conquered the atom, but not our prejudice. We write more, but learn less. We plan more, but accomplish less. We've learned to rush, but not to wait. We build more computers to hold more information, to produce more copies than ever, but we communicate less and less.

These are the times of fast foods and slow digestion, big men and small character, steep profits and shallow relationships. These are the days of two incomes, but more divorce, fancier houses, but broken homes. These are days of quick trips, disposable diapers, throwaway morality, one night stands, overweight bodies, and pills that do everything form cheer, to quiet, to kill. It is a time when there is much in the showroom window and nothing in the stockroom. A time when technology can bring this letter to you, and a time when you can choose either to share this insight, or to just hit delete....

Remember; spend some time with your loved ones, because they are not going to be around forever.

Remember, say a kind word to someone who looks up to you in awe, because that little person soon will grow up and leave your side.

Remember, to give a warm hug to the one next to you, because that is the only treasure you can give with your heart and it doesn't cost a cent.

Remember, to say, 'I Love You' to your partner and your loved ones, but most of all mean it. A kiss and an embrace will mend hurt when it comes from deep inside of you.

Remember to hold hands and cherish the moment for someday that person will not be there again.

Give time to love, give time to speak! And give time to share the precious thoughts in your mind.

AND ALWAYS REMEMBER: Life is not measured by the number of breaths we take, but by the moments that take our breath away

George Carlin

MALE VS FEMALE AT THE ATM MACHINE

A new sign in the Bank Lobby reads:
"Please note that this Bank is installing new Drive-through ATM's enabling customers to withdraw cash without leaving their vehicles. Customers using this new facility are requested to use the procedures outlined below when accessing their accounts. After months of careful research, MALE & FEMALE procedures have been developed. Please follow the appropriate steps for your gender."

MALE PROCEDURE:

1. Drive up to the cash machine.
2. Put down your car window.
3. Insert card into machine and enter PIN.
4. Enter amount of cash required and withdraw.
5. Retrieve card, cash and receipt.
6. Put window up.
7. Drive off.

FEMALE PROCEDURE:

1. Drive up to the cash machine.
2. Reverse and back up the required amount to align car window with the machine.
3. Set parking break, put the window down.
4. Find handbag, remove all contents on to passenger seat to locate card.

5. Tell person on cell phone you will call them back and hang up.

6. Attempt to insert card into machine.

7. Open car door to allow easier access to machine due to its excessive distance from the car.

8. Insert card.

9. Re-insert card the right way.

10. Dig through handbag to find diary with your PIN written on the inside back page.

11. Enter PIN.

12. Press cancel and re-enter correct PIN.

13. Enter amount of cash required.

14. Check makeup in rear view mirror.

15. Retrieve cash and receipt.

16. Empty handbag again to locate wallet and place cash inside.

17. Write debit amount in check register and place receipt in back of checkbook.

18. Re-check makeup.

19. Drive forward 2 feet.

20. Reverse back to cash machine.

21. Retrieve card.

22. Re-empty handbag, locate card holder, and place card into the slot provided!

23. Give dirty look to irate male driver waiting behind you.

24. Restart stalled engine and pull off.

25. Redial person on cell phone.

26. Drive for 2 to 3 miles.

27. Release Parking Brake.

SPAGHETTI

For several years, a man was having an affair with an Italian woman. One night, she confided in him that she was pregnant.

Not wanting to ruin his reputation or his marriage, he would pay her a large sum of money if she would go to Italy to secretly have the child. If she stayed in Italy to raise the child, he would also provide child support until the child turned 18.

She agreed, but asked how he would know when the baby was born. To keep it discrete, he told her to simply mail him a post card, and write "Spaghetti" on the back. He would then arrange for the child support payments to begin.

One day, about 9 months later, he came home to his confused wife, "Honey," she said, "you received a very strange post card today."

"Oh, just give it to me and I'll explain it later," he said.

The wife obeyed and watched as her husband read the card, turned white, and fainted.

On the card was written: "Spaghetti, Spaghetti, Spaghetti, Spaghetti, Spaghetti. Three with meatballs and two without. SEND EXTRA SAUCE!!!

IN HONOR OF STUPID PEOPLE....

In case you needed further proof that the human race is doomed through stupidity, here are some actual label instructions on consumer goods.

On a Sears Hairdryer -- Do not use while sleeping (That's the only time I have to work on my hair.)

On a bag of Fritos -- You could be a winner! No purchase necessary. Details inside. (the shoplifters special?)

On a bar of Dial soap -- "Directions: Use like regular soap." (and that would be???...)

On some Swanson frozen dinners—"Serving suggestions: Defrost." (but, it's just a suggestion.)

On Tesco's Tiramisu dessert (printed on bottom) -- "Do not turn upside down." (well...duh, a bit late, huh!)

On Marks & Spencer Bread Pudding -- "Product will be hot after heating." (...and you thought???...)

On packaging for a Rowena iron - "Do not iron clothes on body." (but wouldn't this save me time?)

On Boot's Children Cough Medicine - "Do not drive a car or operate machinery after taking this medicine. (We could do a lot to reduce the rate of construction accidents if we could just get those 5 year-olds with head-colds off those bulldozers.)

On Nytol Sleep Aid - "Warning: May cause drowsiness." (…I'm thinking this because???...)

On most brands of Christmas lights—"For indoor or outdoor use only." (as opposed to what?)

On a Japanese food processor—"Not to be used for the other use." (now, somebody out there, help me on this. I'm a bit curious.)

On Sainbury's peanuts—"Warning: contains nuts." (talk about a news flash.)

On an American Airlines packet of nuts—"Instructions: Open packet, eat nuts." (Step 3: say what?)

On a child's Superman costume—"Wearing of this garment does not enable you to fly." (I don't blame the company. I blame the parents for this one.)

On a Swedish chainsaw—"do not attempt to stop chain with your hands or genitals." (Oh my God… was there a lot of this happening somewhere?)

AUNT MILDRED

Aging Aunt Mildred was a 93-year old woman who was particularly despondent over the recent death of her husband. She decided that she would just kill herself and join him in death.

Thinking that it would be best to get it over with quickly, she took out his old Army pistol and made the decision to shoot herself in the heart, since it was badly broken in the first place.

Not wanting to miss the vital organ and become a vegetable and a burden to someone, she called her doctor's office to inquire as to just exactly where the heart would be on a woman. The doctor said, "Your heart would be just below your left breast."

Later that night…Mildred was admitted to the hospital with a gunshot wound to her knee.

SCHOOL ANSWERING MACHINE

This is the message that the Pacific Palisades High School (California) staff voted unanimously to record on their school telephone answering machine. This came about because they implemented a policy requiring parents to be responsible for their children's absences and missing homework. The school and teachers are being sued by parents who want their children's failing grades changed to passing grades, even though those children were absent 15 – 30 times during the semester and did not complete enough schoolwork to pass their class. This is the outgoing message:

"Hello! You have reached the automated answering service of your school. In order to assist you in connecting to the right staff member, please listen to all the options before making a selection:

- To lie about why your child is absent – Press 1.

- To make excuses for why your child did not do his work – Press 2.

- To complain about what we do – Press 3.

- To swear at staff members – Press 4.

- To ask why you didn't get information that was already enclosed in your newsletter and several flyers mailed to you – Press 5.

- If you want us to raise your child – Press 6.

- If you want to reach out and touch, slap or hit someone – Press 7.

- To request another teacher, for the third time this year – Press 8.

- To complain about bus transportation – Press 9.

- To complain about school lunches – Press 0.

- If you realize this is the real world and your child must be accountable and responsible for his/her own behavior, class work, homework and that's not the teachers' fault for your child's lack of effort: Hang up and have a nice day!

- If you want this in Spanish, you must be in the wrong country."

DON'T ARGUE WITH THE GAY FLIGHT ATTENDANT

My flight was being served by an obviously gay flight attendant, who seemed to put everyone in a good mood as he served us food and drinks.

As the plane prepared to descend, he came swishing down the aisle and told us, "Captain Marvey has asked me to announce that he'll be landing the big scary plane shortly, so lovely people, if you could just put your trays up, that would be super."

On his trip back up the aisle, he noticed an extremely well-dressed and exotic young woman hadn't moved a muscle. "Perhaps you didn't hear me over those big brute engines, but I asked you to raise your trazy-poo, so the main man can pitty-pat us on the ground.

She calmly turned her head and said, "In my country, I am called a Princess and I take orders from no one."

To which the flight attendant replied, without missing a beat, "Well, sweet-cheeks, in my country I'm called a Queen, so I outrank you. Tray up, Bitch!"

FLORIDA TRUTHS

1. You must first learn to pronounce the name, it is: "FLAAAAARIDA."

2. The morning rush hour is from 5:00 AM to noon. The evening rush hour is from noon to 8:00 PM. Friday's rush hour starts on Thursday morning.

3. The minimum acceptable speed on most freeways is 85 mph. On I-95 your speed is expected to match the highway number. Anything less is grounds to run you off the road while giving you the finger.

4. Forget the traffic rules you learned elsewhere. Florida has its own version of traffic rules. For example, cars/trucks with the loudest muffler go first at a four-way stop: the trucks with the biggest tires go second. However, SUV cell-phone-talking moms ALWAYS have the right of way.

5. If you actually stop at a yellow light, you will be rear ended, cussed out, and possible shot.

6. Never honk at anyone. Ever. Seriously. It's another offense that can get you shot.

7. Road construction is permanent and continuous in Florida. Detour barrels are moved around for your entertainment pleasure during the middle of the night to make the next day's driving a bit more exciting.

8. If someone actually has their turn signal on, wave them to the shoulder immediately to let them know it has been accidentally activated.

9. Merge means race like a madman and cut the person in line off or better yet…run them off the road.

10. For summer driving, it is advisable to wear potholders on your hands.

11. "He needed killin" is a valid defense and don't forget it!

YOU MIGHT BE A FLORIDIAN IF:

- "Down South" means Key West.

- Panhandling" means going to Pensacola.

- You think no-one over 70 should be allowed to drive.

- Flip-flops are everyday wear.

- Shoes are for business meetings and church.

- No, wait, flip flops are good for church too.

- Socks are only for bowling.

- Orange juice from concentrate makes you vomit.

- Tap water makes you vomit.

- Sweet tea can be served at any mean. (Amen)

- An alligator once walked through your neighborhood.

- You smirk when a game show's "Grand Prize" is a trip to Florida.

- You measure distance in minutes.

- You have a drawer full of bathing suits, and one sweatshirt.

- You get annoyed at the tourists who feed seagulls.

- You never use an umbrella because you know the rain will be over in five minutes.

- All the local festivals are named after a fruit.

- A mountain is any hill 100 feet above sea level.

- A good parking place has nothing to do with distance from the store, but everything to do with shade.

- Your winter coat is made of denim.

- You can tell the difference between fire ant bites and mosquito bites.

- You're younger than thirty but some of your friends are over 65.

- You know the four seasons really are: almost summer, summer, not summer but really hot, and Christmas.

- It's not "pop." It's "Coke."

- Anything under 70 degrees is chilly.

- You've hosted a hurricane party.

- You go to a theme park for an afternoon, and know when to get on the best rides.

- You understand the futility of exterminating cockroaches.

- You can pronounce Okeechobee, Kissimmee, Withlacoochee, Okahumpka and Loxahatchee.

- You know where Opa-Lacka Airport is.

- You understand why it's better to have a friend with a boat than have a boat yourself.

- You've driven through Yeehaw Junction.

- Bumper stickers on the pickup in front of you include various fish, the NRA and a confederate flag.

- You were 8 before you realized they made houses without pools.

- You were 12 when you first met someone who couldn't swim.

- You've worn shorts and used the A/C on Christmas.

- You know what the "stingray shuffle" is and why it's important.

- You could swim before you could read.

- You have to drive north to get to The South.

- You dread lovebug season.

- You are on a first name basis with the hurricane list. They aren't Hurricane Charley, Hurricane Frances…but Charley, Frances, Ivan and Jeanne.

- You know what snowbirds are and you hate them!

- You know why flamingos are pink.

- You think a six-foot alligator is actually pretty average!

- You were 12 before you ever saw snow or you still haven't.

BEST OUT OF THE OFFICE AUTO EMAIL RESPONSES

1. I am currently out at a job interview and will reply to you if I fail to get the position. Be prepared for my mood.

2. You are receiving this automatic notification because I am out of the office. If I were in, chances are you wouldn't have received anything at all.

3. Sorry to have missed you, but I am at the doctor's having my brain and heart removed so I can be promoted to our upper management team.

4. I will be unable to delete all the unread, worthless emails you send me until I return from vacation. Please be patient, and your mail will be deleted in the order it was received.

5. Thank you for your email. Your credit card has been charged $5.99 for the first 10 words and $1.99 for each additional word in your message.

6. The email server is unable to verify your server connection and is unable to deliver this message. Please restart your computer and try sending again. (The beauty of this is that when you return, you can see how many in-duh-viduals did this over and over.)

7. Thank you for your message, which has been added to a queuing system. You are currently in 352nd place, and can expect to receive a reply in approximately 19 weeks.

8. Hi, I'm thinking about what you've just sent me. Please wait by your PC for my response.

9. I've run away to join a different circus.

10. I will be out of the office for the next 2 weeks for medical reasons. When I return, please refer to me as 'Loretta' instead of Steve.

BERT AND ERNIE

If you have raised kids (or been one), and gone through the pet syndrome, including toilet flush burials for dead goldfish, the story below will have you laughing out loud!

Overview: I had to take my son's lizard to the vet. Here's what happened:

Just after dinner one night, my son came up to tell me there was "Something wrong" with one of the two lizards he holds prisoner in his room. "He's just lying there looking sick," he told me. "I'm serious, Dad. Can you help?"

I put my best lizard-healer expression on my face and followed him into his bedroom. One of the little lizards was indeed lying on his back, looking stressed. I immediately know what to do. "Honey," I called, "come look at the lizard!"

"Oh, my gosh!" my wife exclaimed, "She's having babies."

"What?" my son demanded, "But their names are Bert and Ernie, Mom!"

I was equally outraged.

"Hey, how can that be? I thought we said we didn't want them to reproduce," I said accusingly to my wife.

"Well, what do you want me to do, post a sign in their cage?" she inquired.

"No, but you were supposed to get two boys!" I reminded her (in my most loving, calm, sweet voice, while gritting my teeth).

"Yeah, Bert and Ernie!" my son agreed.

"Well, it's just a little hard to tell on some guys, you know." She informed me.

By now the rest of the family had gathered to see what was going on. I shrugged, decided to make the best of it.

"Kids, this is going to be a wondrous experience." I announced. "We're about to witness the miracle of birth."

"Oh, gross!" they shrieked.

"Well, isn't THAT just great? What are we going to do with a litter of tiny lizard babies?" my wife wanted to know.

We peered at the patient. After much struggling, what looked like a tiny foot would appear briefly, vanishing a scant second later.

"We don't appear to be making much progress," I noted.

"It's breech." My wife whispered, horrified.

"Do something, Dad!" my son urged.

"Okay, okay." Squeamishly, I reached in and grabbed the foot when it next appeared, giving it a gentle tug. It disappeared. I tried several more times with the same results.

"Should I call 911?" my eldest daughter wanted to know. "Maybe they could talk us through the trauma." (You see a pattern here with the females in my house?)

"Let's get Ernie to the vet," I said grimly. We drove to the vet with my son holding the cage in his lap.

"Breathe, Ernie, breathe," he urged.

"I don't think lizards do Lamaze," his mother noted to him. (Women can be so cruel to their own young. I mean what she does to me is one thing, but this boy is of her womb, for God's sake.).

The vet took Ernie back to the examining room and peered at the little animal through a magnifying glass.

"What do you think, Doc, a C-section?" I suggested scientifically.

"Oh, perfectly," the vet assured us. "This lizard is not in labor. In fact, that isn't EVER going to happen ... Ernie is a boy. You see, Ernie is a young male, and occasionally, as they come into maturity, like most male species, they um ..um..masturbate. Just the way he did, lying on his back." He's blushing, glancing at my wife.

We were silent, absorbing this.

"So, Ernie's just ... just ... excited," my wife offered.

"Exactly," the vet replied, relieved that we understood.

More silence. Then my vicious, cruel wife started to giggle. And giggle. And then even laugh loudly.

"What's so funny?" I demanded, knowing, but not believing that the woman I married would commit the upcoming affront to my flawless manliness.

Tears were now running down her face. "It's just … that… I'm picturing you pulling on its … its …. teeny little.." She gasped for more air to bellow in laughter once more.

"That's enough," I warned. We thanked the vet and hurriedly bundled the lizard and our son back into the car. He was glad everything was going to be okay.

"I know Ernie's really thankful for what you did, Dad." He told me.

"Oh, you have NO idea," my wife agreed, collapsing with laughter.

Two lizards: $140. One cage: $50. Trip to the vet: $30.

Memory of your husband pulling on a lizard's winkie: Priceless!

Moral of the story: Pay attention in biology class. Lizards lay eggs.

THE POLITE WAY TO GO TO THE BATHROOM

During one of her daily classes a teacher trying to teach good manners, asked her students the following question:

"Michael, if you were on a date having dinner with a nice young lady, how would you tell her that you have to go to the bathroom?"

Michael said, "Just a minute, I have to go pee."

The teacher responded by saying, "That would be rude and impolite. What about you Peter, how would you say it?"

Peter said, "I am sorry, but I really need to go to the bathroom. I'll be right back."

"That's better, but still not very nice to say the word bathroom at the dinner table. And you, little Alan, can you use your brain for once and show us your good manners?"

"I would say: Darling, may I please be excused for a moment? I have to shake hands with a very dear friend of mine, whom I hope you'll get to meet after dinner."

WAL-MART GREETER

A very loud, unattractive, mean-acting woman walked into Wal-Mart with her two kids, yelling obscenities at them all the way through the entrance.

The Wal-Mart Greeter said pleasantly "Good morning, and welcome to Wal-Mart. Nice children you have there. Are they twins?"

The ugly woman stopped yelling long enough to say, "Hell no they ain't.

"The oldest one's 9 and the other one's 7. Why the hell would you think they're twins? Are you blind, or just stupid?"

"I'm neither blind nor stupid, Ma'am," replied the greeter, "I just couldn't believe you got laid twice.

"Have a good day and thank you for shopping at Wal-Mart."

A SAINTLY MAN, RECENTLY RETIRED

It is important for men to remember that, as women grow older, it becomes harder for them to maintain the same quality of housekeeping as when they were younger. When you notice this, try not to yell at them. Some are oversensitive, and there's nothing worse than an oversensitive woman.

My name is Jim. Let me relate how I handled the situation with my wife, Peggy. When I retired a few years ago, it became necessary for Peggy to get a full-time job along with her part-time job, both for extra income and for the health benefits that we needed.

Shortly after she started working, I noticed she was beginning to show her age. I usually get home from the golf club about the same time she gets home from work. Although she knows how hungry I am, she almost always says she has to rest for half an hour or so before she starts dinner. I don't yell at her. Instead, I tell her to take her time and just wake me when she gets dinner on the table. I generally have lunch in the Men's Grill at the club so eating out is not reasonable. I'm ready for some home-cooked grub when I hit that door.

She used to do the dishes as soon as we finished eating. But now it's not unusual for them to sit on the table for several hours after dinner. I do what I can by diplomatically reminding her several times each evening that they won't clean themselves. I know she really appreciates this, as it does seem to motivate her to get them done before she goes to bed.

Another symptom of aging is complaining, I think. For example, she will say that it is difficult for her to find time to pay the monthly bills during her lunch hour. But, boys, we take 'em for better or worse, so I just smile and offer encouragement. I tell her to stretch it out over two or even three days. That way she won't have to rush so much. I also remind her that missing lunch completely now and then wouldn't hurt her any (if you know what I mean). I like to think tact is one of my strong points.

When doing simple jobs, she seems to think she needs more rest periods. She had to take a break when she was only half-finished mowing the yard. I try not to make a scene. I'm a fair man. I tell her to fix herself a nice, big, cold glass of freshly squeezed lemonade and just sit for a while. And, as long as she is making one for herself, she may as well make one for me too.

I know that I probably look like a saint in the way I support Peggy. I'm not saying that showing this much consideration is easy. Many men will find it difficult. Some will find it impossible! Nobody knows better than I do how frustrating women get as they get older. However, guys, even if you just use a little more tact and less criticism of your aging wife because of this article, I will consider that writing it was well worthwhile. After all, we are put on this earth to help each other.

Signed, Jim

Editor's Note: Jim died suddenly on May 27 of a perforated rectum. The police report says he was found with a Calloway extra-long 50-inch Big Bertha Driver II golf club jammed up his rear end, with barely 5 inches of grip showing and a sledgehammer lying nearby.

His wife Peggy was arrested and charged with murder. The all-woman jury took only 15 minutes to find her Not Guilty, accepting her defense that Jim somehow, without looking, accidentally sat down on his golf club.

GEORGE CARLIN'S NEW RULES FOR 2007

New Rule: Stop giving me that pop-up ad for classmates.com! There's a reason you don't talk to people for 25 to 30 years. Because you don't particularly like them! Besides, I already know what the captain of the football team is doing these days, he's mowing my lawn.

New Rule: Don't eat anything that's served to you out of a window unless you're a seagull. People are acting all shocked that a human finger was found in a bowl of Wendy's chili. Hey, it cost less than a dollar. What did you expect it to contain? Caviar?

New Rule: If you need to shave and you still collect baseball cards, you're a dope. If you're a kid, the cards are keepsakes of your idols. If you're a grown man, they're pictures of men.

New Rule: Ladies, leave your eyebrows alone. Here's how much men care about four eyebrows: do you have two of them? Okay, we're done.

New Rule: There's no such thing as flavored water. There's a whole aisle of this crap at the supermarket – water, but without that watery taste. Sorry, but flavored water is called a soft drink. You want flavored water? Pour some scotch over ice and let it melt. That's your flavored water.

New Rule: Stop screwing with old people. Target is introducing a redesigned pill bottle that's square, with a bigger label. And the top is not the bottom. And by the time grandpa figures out how to open it, his ass will be in the morgue. Congratulations, Target, you just solved the Social Security crisis.

New Rule: I'm not the cashier! By the time I look up from figuring which way to slide my card, entering my PIN number, finding the pressing "Enter," verifying the amount, deciding, no, I don't want cash back, and pressing "Enter" again, the kid who is supposed to be ringing me up is standing there eating my candy bar.

New Rule: Just because your tattoo has Chinese characters in it doesn't make you spiritual. It's right above the crack of your ass. And it translates to "chicken with broccoli." The last time you did anything spiritual, you were praying to God you weren't pregnant. You're not spiritual. You're just high.

New rule: Competitive eating isn't a sport. It's one of the seven deadly sins. ESPN recently televised the U.S. Open of Competitive Eating, because watching those celebrities playing poker was just too damned exciting. What's next, competitive farting? Oh no wait! They're already doing that. It's called "The Howard Stern Show."

New Rule: I don't need a bigger mega M&M's. If I'm extra hungry for M&M's I'll go nuts and eat two.

New Rule: If you're going to insist on making movies based on crappy, old television shows, then you have to give everyone in the Cineplex a remote so we can see what's playing on the other screens. Let's remember the reason something was a television show in the first place is that the idea wasn't good to be a movie.

New Rule: No more gift registries. You know, it used to be just for weddings. Not it's for babies and new homes, graduations and getting out of rehab. Picking out the stuff you want and having other people buy it for you isn't gift giving, it's the white people's version of looting.

New Rule: And this one is long overdue: No more bathroom attendants. After I zip up, some guy is offering me a towel and a mint like I just had sex with George Michael. I can't even tell if he's supposed to be there, or just some freak with a fetish. I don't want to be on your web cam, dude. I just want to wash my hands.

New Rule: When I ask how old your toddler is, I don't need to know months. "27 months." "He's two," will do just fine. And I don't really care in the first place.

New Rule: If you ever hope to be a credible adult and want a job that pays better than minimum wage, then for God's sake don't pierce or tattoo every available piece of flesh. If so, then plan your future around saying "Do you want fries with that?"

NICE DAILY DOSE OF HUMOR

When I was born, I was BLACK,
When I grew up I was BLACK,
When I went in the sun, I stayed BLACK,
When I got cold, I was BLACK,
When I was scared, I was BLACK,
When I was sick, I was Black,
And when I die, I'll still be BLACK.

Now, you "white" folks…
When you're born, you're PINK,
When you grow-up, you're White,
When you go in the sun, you get RED,
When you're cold, you turn BLUE,
When you're scared, you're YELLOW,
When you get sick, you're GREEN,
When you bruise, you turn PURPLE,
And when you die, you look GRAY.

So who y'all callin' COLORED folks?

9 WORDS WOMEN USE

FINE: This is the word women use to end an argument when they are right and you need to shut up.

FIVE MINUTES: If she is getting dressed, this means a half an hour. Five minutes is only five minutes if you have just been given five more minutes to watch the game before helping around the house.

NOTHING: This is the calm before the storm. This means something, and you should be on your toes. Arguments that begin with nothing usually end in fine.

GO AHEAD: This is a dare, not permission. Don't Do It!

LOUD SIGH: This is not actually a word, but is a non-verbal statement often misunderstood by men. A loud sign means she thinks you are an idiot and wonders why she is wasting her time standing here and arguing with you about nothing. (Refer back to #3 for the meaning of nothing.)

THAT"S OKAY: This is one of the most dangerous statements a woman can make to a man. That's okay means she wants to think long and hard before deciding how and when you will pay for your mistake.

THANKS: A woman is thanking you, do not question, or Faint. Just say you're welcome.

WHATEVER: Is a women's way of saying F&@% YOU!

DON'T WORRY ABOUT IT, I GOT IT: Another dangerous statement, meaning this is something that a woman has told a man to do several times, but is now doing it herself. This will later result in a man asking "What's wrong?" For the woman's response refer to #3.

DRINKING WITH A REDNECK GIRL.

A Mexican, an Iraqi, and a redneck girl are in the same bar. When the Mexican finishes his beer, he throws his glass in the air, pulls out his pistol, and shoots the glass to pieces. He says, "In Mexico our glasses are so cheap we don't need to drink with the same one twice."

The Iraqi, obviously impressed by this, drinks his beer, throws his glass into the air, pulls out his AK-47, and shoots the glass to pieces. He says, "In Iraq we have so much sand to make glasses that we don't need to drink with the same one twice either."

The redneck girl, cool as a cucumber, picks up her beer, downs it in on draft, throws the glass into the air, whips out her 45, and shoots the Mexican and the Iraqi. Catching the glass, setting it on the bar, and calling for a refill, she says, "In America we have so many illegal Mexicans and Arabs that we don't have to drink with the same ones twice."

THE WINNER

This beautiful, well-endowed, shapely young blonde arrives at her course alone and joins a threesome of men. All through the round, with the help of tips from the three men, she arrives at the 18th hole at 98 with only a 6-foot putt left to break 100.

She tells the men, "I have never broken 100 since I started playing golf two years ago, I am so anxious to break 100, that whichever one of you men gives me the best tip as to how to sink this putt, I will reward him by making love to him right here on the green. He will enjoy it so much that he will remember it, and tell all his friends the ecstasy he experienced for the rest of his life."

The first guy checks the line and break from all sides and suggests that she borrow three inches right of the hole and just stroke it hard enough to drop it in the hole.

The second guy agrees, but tells her to hit it firmly and slam-dunk it in the hole.

She looks around for the third guy and finds him frantically undressing right down to his birthday suit. She asks him what on earth he is doing. He replies he has won the love making session. She tells him he hasn't even given her his tip.

To this he replies, "Pick it up; it's a gimmee."

CHEAP LABOR... CHEAP TOMATOES...

This should make everyone think, be you Democrat, Republican or Independent!

From a California school teacher - - - "As you listen to the news about the student protests over illegal immigration, there are some things that you should be aware of:

I am in charge of the English-as-a-second language department at a large southern California high school which is designated a Title 1 school, meaning that its students average lower socioeconomic and income levels.

Most of the schools you are hearing about, South Gate High, Bell Gardens, Huntington Park, etc., where these students are protesting, are also Title 1 school.

Title 1 schools are on the free breakfast and free lunch program. When I say free breakfast, I'm not talking a glass of milk and roll - - but a full breakfast and cereal bar with fruits and juices that would make a Marriott proud. The waste of this food is monumental, with trays and trays of it being dumped in the trash uneaten. (OUR TAX DOLLARS AT WORK.)

It was estimated that well over 50% of these students are obese or at least moderately overweight. About 75% or more DO have cell phones. The school also provides day care centers for the unwed teenage pregnant girls (some as young as 13) so they can attend class without the inconvenience of having to arrange for babysitters or having family watch their kids. (OUR TAX DOLLARS AT WORK)

I was ordered to spend $700,000 on my department or risk losing funding for the upcoming year even though there was little need for anything; my budget was already substantial. I ended up buying new computers for the computer learning center, half of which, one month later, have been carved with graffiti by the appreciative students who obviously feel humbled and grateful to have a free education in America. (OUR TAX DOLLAR AT WORK)

I have had to intervene several times for young and substitute teachers whose classes consist of many illegal immigrants students here in the country less than 3 months who raised so much hell with the female teachers, calling them "Putas" whores and throwing things that the teacher were in tears.

Free medical, free education, free food, day care etc., etc., etc. Is it any wonder they feel entitled to not only be in this country but to demand rights, privileges and entitlements?

To those who want to point out how much these illegal immigrants contribute to our society because they like their gardener and housekeeper and they like to pay less for tomatoes; spend some time in the real world of illegal immigration and see the TRUE costs.
Higher insurance, medical facilities closing, higher medical costs, more crime, lower standards of education in our schools, overcrowding, new diseases etc., etc. For me, I'll pay more for tomatoes.

We need to wake up. The guest worker program will be a disaster because we won't have the guts to enforce it.

Does anyone in their right mind really think they will voluntarily leave and return?

There are many hardworking Hispanic/American citizens that contribute to our country and many that I consider my true friends.

We should encourage and accept those Hispanics who have done it the right and legal way.

It does, however, have everything to do with culture: A third-world culture that does not value education, that accepts children getting pregnant and dropping out of school by 15 and that refuses to assimilate, and an American culture that has become so weak and worried about "politically correct" that we don't have the will to do anything about it.

If this makes your blood boil, as it did mine, forward this to everyone you know.

Cheap Labor? Isn't that what the whole immigration issue is about? Business doesn't want to pay a decent wage. Consumers don't want expensive produce. Government will tell you Americans don't want the jobs. But the bottom line is cheap labor. The phrase "cheap labor" is a myth, a farce, and a lie. There is no such thing as 'cheap labor."

Take for example, an illegal alien with a wife and five children. He takes a job for $5.00 or $6.00 per hour. At that wage, with six dependents, he pays no income tax, yet at the end of the year, if he files an Income tax Return, he gets an "earned income credit" of up to $3,200 free.

He qualifies for Section 8 housing and subsidized rent. He qualifies for food stamps. He qualifies for free (no deductible, no co-pay) health care. His children get free breakfasts and lunches at school. He requires bilingual teachers and books. He qualifies for relief from high energy bills.

If they are or become, aged, blind or disabled, they qualify for SSI. Once qualified for SSI they can qualify for Medicare. All of this is at (our) taxpayer's expense.

He doesn't worry about car insurance, life insurance, or homeowners insurance. Taxpayers provide Spanish language signs, bulletins and printed material. He and his family receive the equivalent of $20 to $30 per hour in benefits.

Working Americans are lucky to have $5.00 or $6.00 per hour left after paying their bills and his. The American taxpayers also pay for increased crime, graffiti and trash clean-up.

Cheap labor? YEAH RIGHT! Wake up people. THESE ARE THE QUESTIONS WE SHOULD BE ADDRESSING TO THE PREDIDENTIAL CANDIDATES FOR EITHER PARTY. AND WHEN THEY LIE TO US AND DON'T DO AS THEY SAY, WE SHOULD REPLACE THEM AT ONCE.

20 WAYS TO MAINTAIN
A HEALTHY LEVEL OF INSANITY

1. At lunch time, sit in your parked car with sunglasses on and point a hair dryer at passing cars. See if they slow down.

2. Page yourself over the intercom. Don't disguise your voice.

3. Every time someone asks you to do something, ask if they want fries with that.

4. Put your garbage can on your desk and label it "In."

5. Put decaf in the coffee maker for 3 weeks. Once everyone has gotten over their caffeine addictions, switch to Espresso.

6. In the Memory Field of all your checks, write, "For Smuggling Drugs."

7. Finish all your sentences with "In accordance with the Prophecy."

8. Don't use any punctuation.

9. As often as possible, skip rather than walk.

10. Order a diet water whenever you go out to eat, with a serious face.

11. Specify that your drive-through order is "To Go."

12. Sing along at the opera.

13. Go to a poetry recital. And ask why the poems don't rhyme?

14. Put mosquito netting around your work area, and play tropical sounds all day.

15. Five days in advance, tell your friends you can't attend their party because you're not in the mood.

16. Have your co-workers address you by your wrestling name, Rock Bottom.

17. When the money comes out the ATM, scream "I Won! I Won!"

18. When leaving the zoo, start running towards the parking lot, yelling "Run for your lives! They're loose!"

19. Tell your children over dinner, "Due to the economy, we are going to have to let one of you go."

20. And the final way to keep a healthy level of insanity…. Send this e-mail to someone to make them smile.

It's called…therapy!

NO NURSING HOME FOR US!

We are checking into the Holiday Inn! With the average cost for a nursing home care costing $188 per day, there is a better way when we get old and feeble.

We have already checked on reservations at the Holiday Inn. For a combined long term stay discount and senior discount, it's $49.23 per night. That leaves $128.77 a day for: breakfast, lunch and dinner in any restaurant we want. And it includes room service, laundry, gratuities and special TV movies. Plus, they provide a swimming pool, a workout room, a lounge and washer-dryer, etc. Most have free toothpaste and razors, and all have free shampoo and soap.

$5 worth of tips a day will have the entire staff scrambling to help you. They treat you like a customer, not a patient. There is a city bus stop out front, and seniors ride free. The handicap bus will also pick you up (if you fake a decent limp).

To meet other nice people, call a church bus on Sundays.

For a change of scenery, take the airport shuttle bus and eat at one of the nice restaurants there. While you're at the airport, fly somewhere. Otherwise, the cash keeps building up.

It takes months to get into decent nursing homes. Holiday Inn will take your reservation today. And you are not stuck in one place forever, you can move from Inn to Inn, or even from city to city. Want to see Hawaii? They have a Holiday Inn there too.

TV broken? Light bulbs need changing? Need a mattress replaced? No problem. Then fix everything, and apologize for the inconvenience.

The Inn has a night security person and daily room service. The maid checks to see if you are ok, they will call the undertaker or an ambulance. If you fall and break a hip, Medicare will pay for the hip, and Holiday Inn will upgrade you to a suite for the rest of your life.

And no worries about visits from family. They will always be glad to find you, and probably check in for a few days mini-vacation.

The grandkids can use the pool. What more can you ask for? So, when we reach that golden age, we'll face it with a grin.

UPDATE ON JOE ARPAIO

To those of you not familiar with Joe Arpaio, he is the Maricopa Arizona County Sheriff, and he keeps getting elected over and over again.

This is one of the reasons why: Sheriff Joe Arpaio, in Arizona, who created the "Tent City Jail";

He has jail meals down to 40 cents a serving (actually 20 cents) and charges the inmates for them.

He stopped smoking and porno magazines in the jail. Took away their weights, and cut off all but "G rated movies.

He started chain gangs so the inmates could do free work on county and city projects. Then he started chain gangs for women so he wouldn't get sued for discrimination.

He took away cable TV until he found out there was a federal court order that requires cable TV for jails. So he hooked up the cable TV again, only let the Disney Channel and the Weather Channel available. When asked why the weather channel, he replied, "so they will know how hot it's gonna be while they are working on my chain gangs."

He cut off coffee since it has zero nutritional value. When the inmates complained, he told them, "This isn't the Ritz/Carlton. If you don't like it, don't come back."

He bought Newt Gingrich's lecture series on videotape that he pipes into the jail. When asked by a reporter if he had any lecture series by a

Democrat, he replied that a democratic lecture series might explain why a lot of the inmates were in his jails in the first place.

With temperatures being even hotter than usual in Phoenix (116 degrees just set a new record). The Associated Press Reports: About 2,000 inmates living in a barbed-wire-surrounded tent encampment at the Maricopa County Jail have been given permission to strip down to their government issued pink boxer shorts.

On Wednesday, hundreds of men wearing boxers were either curled up on their bunk beds or chatted in the tents, which reached 138 degrees inside the tents the week before.

Many were also swathed in wet, pink towels as sweat collected on their chests and dripped down to their pink socks. "It feels like we are in a furnace," said James Aanzot, an inmate who has lived in the tents for 1 year. "It's inhumane."

Joe Arpaio, the tough-guy sheriff who created the tent city and long ago started making his prisoners wear pink, and eat bologna sandwiches, is not one bit sympathetic. He said that he told all of the inmates: "It's 120 degrees in Iraq and our soldiers are living in tents too, and they have to wear full battle gear, but they didn't commit any crimes, so shut your damned mouths!"

Maybe if all prisons were like this one, there would be a lot less crime and/or repeat offenders.

Sheriff Joe.

BEER TROUBLESHOOTING GUIDE

1. Symptom: Feet cold and wet.

    Cause: Glass being held at incorrect angle.

    Corrective Action: Rotate glass so that open end points toward ceiling.

2. Symptom: Feet warm and wet.

    Cause: Improper bladder control.

    Corrective Action: Stand next to the nearest dog, complain about lack of house training.

3. Symptom: Beer usually pale and tasteless.

    Cause: A. Glass empty. B. You're holding a Coors Lite.

    Corrective Action: Get someone to buy you another beer.

4. Symptom: Opposite wall covered with fluorescent lights.

    Cause: You have fallen over backward.

    Corrective Action: Have yourself lashed to bar.

5. Symptom: Mouth contains cigarette butts, back of head covered with ashes.

    Cause: You have fallen forward.

    Corrective Action: See #4 above.

6. Symptom: Beer tasteless, front of you shirt is wet.

    Cause: A. Mouth not open, B. Glass applied to wrong part of face.

Corrective Actions: Retire to restroom, practice in mirror.

7. Symptom: Floor blurred.

    Cause: You are looking through bottom of empty glass.

    Corrective Action: Get someone to buy you another beer.

8. Symptom: Floor moving.

    Cause: You are being carried out.

    Corrective Action: Find out if you are being taken to another bar.

9. Symptom: Room seems unusually dark.

    Cause: Bar has closed.

    Corrective Action: Confirm home address with bartender. If staff is gone, grab a six-pack to go and hit the nearest fire escape door. Run.

10. Symptom: Taxi suddenly takes on colorful aspect and textures.

    Cause: Beer consumption has exceeded personal limitations.

    Corrective Action: Cover mouth, open window, stick head outside.

11. Symptom: Everyone looks up to you and smiles.

    Cause: You are dancing on the table.

    Corrective Action: Fall on someone cushy-looking.

12. Symptom: Beer is crystal-clear.

    Cause: Its water! Somebody is trying to sober you up.

    Corrective Action: Punch him.

13. Symptom: People are standing around urinals, talking or putting on makeup.

Cause: You're in the ladies room.

Corrective Action: Do not use urinal! Excuse yourself, exit and try the next door down the hall. Try to get phone numbers (optional).

14. Symptom: Hands hurt, nose hurts, mind unusually clear.

    Cause: You have been in a fight.

    Corrective Action: Apologize to everyone you see, just in case it was them.

15. Symptom: Don't recognize anyone; don't recognize the room you're in.

    Cause: You've wandered into the wrong party.

    Corrective Action: See if they have free beer.

16. Symptom: Your bedroom is painted gray, has a concrete floor and an interesting steel door. Toilet may be conveniently located next to your bunk.

    Cause: A. You're in jail, B. You're in the navy.

    Corrective Action: Sleep it off, you can always get out tomorrow. Don't talk to your new roommate, and under no circumstances sleep on your stomach.

17. Symptom: You are dancing to a Village People song, and your partner is wearing leather chaps.

    Cause: You're in a gay bar.

    Corrective Action: Keeping your back to the wall, edge toward nearest exit. Do not accept offers for backrubs.

18. Symptom: Your singing sounds distorted.

    Cause: The beer is too weak.

Corrective Action: Have more beer until your voice improves.

19. Symptom: Don't remember the words to the song.

Cause: Beer is just right.

Corrective Action: Play air guitar.

A SIMPLE TEST

This test only has one question, but it's a very important one. By giving an honest answer, you will discover where you stand 'morally.' The test features an unlikely, completely-fictional situation in which you will have to make a decision. Remember that your answer needs to be honest, yet spontaneous.

The Situation:

You are in Florida, Miami to be specific. There is chaos all around you caused by a hurricane with severe flooding. This is a flood of Biblical proportions. You are photojournalist working for a major newspaper, and you're caught in the middle of this epic disaster. The situation is nearly hopeless.

You're trying to shoot career making photos. There are houses and people swirling-around you, some disappearing under the water. Nature is unlashing all of its destructive fury.

The Test:

Suddenly, you see a woman in the water. She is fighting for her life, trying not to be taken down with the debris. You move closer. Somehow, the woman looks familiar. You suddenly realize who it is. It's Hillary Clinton!

At the same time, you notice that the raging waters are about to take her under forever. You have two options: You can save the life of Hillary Clinton or you can shoot a dramatic Pulitzer Prize winning photo, documenting the death of one of the world's most powerful women.

The Question:

Here's the question, and please give an honest answer....

Would you select high contrast color film, or would you go with the classic simplicity of black-and-white?

THOSE BORN 1930 – 1979 (MUST READ)

First, we survived being born to mothers who smoked and/or drank while they were pregnant.

They took aspirin, ate blue cheese dressing, tuna from a can, and didn't get tested for diabetes.

Then after that trauma, we were put to sleep on our tummies in baby cribs covered with bright colored led-based paints.

We had no childproof lids on medicine bottles, doors or cabinets and when we rode our bikes, we had no helmets, not to mention, the risks we took hitchhiking.

As infants and children, we would ride in cars with no car seats, booster seats, seat belts or air bags.

Riding in the back of a pick up on a warm day was always special treat.

We drank water from the garden hose and NOT from a bottle.

We shared one soft drink with four friends, from one bottle and NO ONE actually died from this.

We ate cupcakes, white bread and real butter, and drank Kool-Aid made with sugar, but we weren't overweight because WE WERE ALWAYS OUTSIDE PLAYING!

We would leave home in the morning and play all day, as long as we were back when the streetlights came on.

No one was able to reach us all day. AND we were OK.

We would spend hours building our go-carts out of scraps and then ride down the hill, only to find out we forgot the brakes. After running into the bushes a few times, we learned to solve the problem.

We did not have Playstations, Nintendos, X-Boxes, no video games at all, no 150 channels on cable, no video movies or DVDs, no surround-sound or CDs, no cell phones, no personal computers, no Internet or chat rooms....WE HAD FRIENDS and we went outside and found them!

We fell out of trees, got cut, broke bones and teeth and there were no lawsuits from these accidents.

We ate worms and mud pies made from dirt, and the worms did not live in us forever.

We were given BB guns for our 10th birthdays, made up games with sticks and tennis balls and, although we were told it would happen, we did not put out very many eyes.

We rode bikes or walked to a friend's house and knocked on the door or rang the bell, or just walked in and talked to them!

Little League had tryouts and not everyone made the team. Those who didn't had to learn to deal with disappointment. Imagine that!!

The idea of a parent bailing us out if we broke the law was unheard of. They actually sided with the law!

These generations have produced some of the best risk-takers, problem solvers and inventors ever!

The past 50 years have been an explosion of innovation and new ideas. We had freedom, failure, success and responsibility, and we learned HOW TO DEAL WITH IT!

If you are one of them, CONGRATULATIONS! You might want to share this with others who have had the luck to grow up as kids, before the lawyers and the government regulated so much of our lives **for our own good**.

While you are at it, forward this to your kids so they will know how brave (and lucky) their parents were. Kind of makes you want to run through the house with scissors, doesn't it?!

The quote of the month is by Jay Leno: "With hurricanes, tornados, fires out of control, mud slides, flooding, severe thunderstorms tearing up the country from one end to another, and with the threat of bird flu and terrorist attacks, are we sure this is a good time to take God out of the Pledge of Allegiance?"

WISDOM FROM LARRY THE CABLE GUY

- A day without sunshine is like night.

- On the other hand, you have different fingers.

- 42.7% of all statistics are made up on the spot.

- 99% of lawyers give the rest a bad name.

- Remember, half of the people you know are below average.

- He, who laughs last, thinks slowest.

- Depression is merely anger without enthusiasm.

- The early bird may get the worm, but the second mouse gets the cheese in the trap.

- Support bacteria. They're the only culture some people have.

- A clear conscience is usually the sign of a bad memory.

- Change is inevitable, except from vending machines.

- If you think nobody cares, try missing a couple payments.

- How many of you believe in psycho-kinesis? Raise your hand.

- OK, so what's the speed of dark?

- When everything is coming your way, you're in the wrong lane.

- Hard work pays off in the future. Laziness pays off now.

- How much deeper would the ocean be without sponges?

- Eagles may soar, but weasels don't get sucked into jet engines.

- What happens if you get scared half to death, twice?

- Why do psychics have to ask you for your name?

- Inside every older person is a younger person wondering, "What the heck happened?"

- Just remember – if the world didn't suck, we would all fall off.

- Light travels faster than sound. That's why some people appear bright until you hear them speak.

- Life isn't like a box of chocolates. It's more like a jar of jalapenos. What you do today might burn your butt tomorrow.

SOUTHWEST AIRLINES

A mother and her 6 year old son were flying Southwest Airlines from Kansas City to Chicago.

The son (who had been looking out the window) turned to his mother and asked, "If big dogs have baby dogs and big cats have baby cats, why don't big planes have baby planes?"

The mother, who couldn't think of an answer, told her son to ask the stewardess.

So the boy walks to the galley and asks the stewardess, "If big dogs have baby dogs, and big cats have baby cats, why don't big planes have baby planes?"

The stewardess responded, "Did your mother tell you to ask me?"

The boy said, "Yes, she did…."

"Well then, tell your mother that there are no baby planes because Southwest always pulls out on time. Have your mother explain that to you."

CONSPIRACY

This kind of stuff has got to STOP. We must stop this IMMEDIATELY!

- Have you noticed that stairs are getting steeper? Groceries are heavier. And, everything is farther away. Yesterday I walked to the corner and I was dumbfounded to discover how long our street has become! This extension work was apparently done at night! Very sneaky stuff....

- And, you know, people are less considerate now, especially the youngsters. They speak in whispers all the time! If you ask them to speak up they just keep repeating themselves, endlessly mouthing the same silent message until they're red in the face! What do they think I am a lip reader?

- I also think they are much younger than I was at the same age. On the other hand, people my own age are so much older than I am. I ran into an old friend the other day, and she has aged so much that she didn't even recognize me.

- Another thing, everyone drives so fast these days! You're risking life and limb if you happen to pull onto the freeway in front of them. All I can say is, their brakes must wear out awfully fast, the way I see them screech and swerve in my rear view mirror.

- Clothing manufactures are less civilized these days. Why else would they suddenly start labeling a size 32 pair of pants a 42, or medium shirt as 'extra large'? A size 6 skirt a 10 or a small sweater as large? Do they think no one notices that these things no longer fit around the waist, hips, thighs, and neck?

- The people who make bathroom scales are pulling the same prank, but in reverse. Do they think I actually "believe" the number I see on that dial? Heck! I would never let myself weigh that much! Just who do these people think they're fooling?

- I'd like to call up someone in authority to report what's going on – but the telephone company is in on the conspiracy too: they've printed the phone books in such small type that no one could ever find a number in there!

- All I can do is pass along this warning: We are under attack! Unless something drastic happens, pretty soon everyone will have to suffer these awful indignities.

Please pass this on to everyone you know as soon as possible so we can get this conspiracy stopped!

P.S.: I am sending this to you in a larger font size, because something has caused my computer's regular fonts to be smaller than they once were. (They must be sneaking to my house and messing around with my computer. Probably CIA...!!!) Pretty scary stuff huh?

IMMIGRANTS, NOT AMERICANS, MUST ADAPT

I am tired of this nation worrying about whether we ore offending some individual or their culture. Since the terrorist attacks on Sept. 11, we have experienced a surge in patriotism by the majority of Americans. However, the dust from the attacks had barely settled when the "politically correct!" crowd began complaining about the possibility that our patriotism was offending others.

I am not against immigration, nor do I hold a grudge against anyone who is seeking a better life by coming to America. Our population is almost entirely made up of descendants of immigrants. However, there are a few things that those who have recently come to our country, and apparently some born here, need to understand.

This idea of America being a multicultural communist has served only to dilute our sovereignty and our national identity. As Americans...,we have our own culture, our own society, our own language and our own lifestyle. This culture has been developed over centuries of struggles, trials, and victories by millions of men and women who have sought freedom.

We speak ENGLISH, not Spanish, Portuguese, Arabic, Chinese, Japanese, Russian, or any other language. Therefore, if you wish to become part of our society, learn the language!

"In God We Trust" is our national motto. This is not some Christian, right wing, political slogan. We adopted this motto because Christian men and women...on Christian principles...founded this nation...and this is clearly documented.

It is certainly appropriate to display it on the walls of our schools. If God offends you, then I suggest you consider another part of the world as your new home...because God is part of our culture.

If Stars and Stripes offend you, or you don't like Uncle Sam, then you should seriously consider a move to another part of this planet.

We are happy with our culture and have no desire to change, and we really don't care how you did things where you came from. This is OUR COUNTRY, our land, and our lifestyle.

Our First Amendment gives every citizen the right to express his opinion and we will allow you every opportunity to do so! But once you are done complaining...whining...and griping...about our flag... our pledge...our national motto...or our way of life...I highly encourage you to take advantage of one other Great American Freedom...The Right To Leave!

DADDY'S RULES FOR DATING

Rule One: If you pull into my driveway and honk you'd better be delivering a package, because you're sure not picking anything up.

Rule Two: You do not touch my daughter in front of me. You may glance at her, so long as you do not peer at anything below her neck. If you cannot keep your eyes or hands off of my daughter's body, I will remove them.

Rule Three: I am aware that it is considered fashionable for boys of your age to wear their trousers so loosely that they appear to be falling off your hips. Please don't take this as an insult, but you and all of your friends are complete idiots. Still, I want to be fair and open minded about this issue, so I propose this compromise: You may come to the door with your underwear showing and your pants ten sizes too big, and I will not object. However, in order to ensure that your clothes do not, in fact come off during the course of your date with my daughter, I will take my nail gun and fasten your trousers securely in place to your waist before you leave my house.

Rule Four: I'm sure you've been told that in today's world, sex without utilizing a 'Barrier method' of some kind can kill you. Let me elaborate, when it comes to sex, I am the barrier, and I will kill you.

Rule Five: It is usually understood that in order for us to get to know each other, we should talk about sports, politics, and other issues of the day. Please do not do this. The only information I require from you is an indication of when you expect to have my daughter safely back at my house, and the only word I need from you on this subject is: 'early.'

Rule Six: I have no doubt you are a popular fellow, with many opportunities to date other girls. This is fine with me as long as it is okay with my daughter. Otherwise, once you have gone out with my little girl, you will continue to date no one but her until she is finished with you. If you make her cry, I will make you cry.

Rule Seven: As you stand in my front hallway, waiting for my daughter to appear, and more than an hour goes by, do not sigh and fidget. If you want to be on time for the movie, you should not be dating. My daughter is putting on her makeup, a process that can take longer than painting the Golden Gate Bridge. Instead of just standing there, why don't you do something useful, like changing the oil in my car?

Rule Eight: The following places are not appropriate for a date with my daughter: Places where there are beds, sofas, or anything softer than a wooden stool. Places where there is darkness. Places where there is dancing, holding hands, or happiness Places where the ambient temperature is warm enough to induce my daughter to wear shorts, tank tops, midriff T-shirts, or anything other than overalls, a sweater, and a goose down parka – zipped up to her throat. Movies with strong romantic or sexual themes are to be avoided; movies which feature chain saws are okay. Hockey games are okay. Old folks homes are better.

Rule Nine: Do not lie to me. I may appear to be a potbellied, balding, middle-aged, dimwitted has-been. But on issues relating to my daughter, I am the all-knowing, merciless God of your universe. If I ask you where you are going and with whom, you have one chance to tell me the truth, the whole truth and nothing but the truth. I have a shotgun, a shovel, and five acres of land behind my house. Do not trifle with me.

Rule Ten: Be afraid. Be very afraid. It takes very little for me to mistake the sound of your car in the driveway for a chopper coming in over a rice paddy near Hanoi. When my Agent Orange starts acting up, the voices in my head frequently tell me to clean the guns, as I wait for you to bring my daughter home. As soon as you pull into the driveway you should exit the car with both hands in plain sight. Speak the perimeter password, announce in a clear voice that you have brought my daughter home safely and early, then return to your car – there is no need for you to come inside. The camouflaged face at the window is mine.

LOUISIANA TITLE SEARCH

New Orleans residents are challenged often with the task of tracing home titles back potentially hundreds of years. With a community rich with history stretching back over two centuries, houses have been passed along through generations of family, making it quite difficult to establish ownership.

Here's a great letter an attorney wrote to the FHA on behalf of a client that I thought was absolutely priceless....

A New Orleans lawyer sought an FHA loan for a client. He was told the loan would be granted if he could prove satisfactory title to a parcel of property being offered as collateral. The title to the property dated back to 1803, which took the lawyer three months to track down. After sending the information to the FHA, he received the following reply....

"Upon review of you letter adjoining your client's loan application, we note that the request is supported by an Abstract of Title. While we compliment the able manner in which you have prepared and presented the application, we must point out that you have only cleared title to the proposed collateral property back to 1803. Before final approval can be accorded, it will be necessary to clear the title back to its origin."

Annoyed, the lawyer responded as follows...
"Your letter regarding title in Case No. 189156 has been received. I note that you wish to have title extended further than the 194 years covered by the present application. I was unaware that any educated person in this country, particularly those working in the property area,

would not know that Louisiana was purchased, by the U.S., from France in 1803, the year of origin identified in our application.

"For the education of uninformed FHA bureaucrats…, the title to the land prior to U.S. ownership was obtained from France, which had acquired it by Right of Conquest from Spain.

"The land came into the possession of Spain by Right of Discovery made in the year 1492 by a sea captain named Christopher Columbus, who had been granted the privilege of seeking a new route to India by the Spanish monarch, Isabella.

"The good queen, Isabella, being a pious woman and almost as careful about Titles as the FHA, took the precaution of securing the blessing of the Pope before she sold her jewels to finance Columbus expedition.

"Now the Pope, as I'm sure you may know, is the emissary of Jesus Christ, the Son of God, and God, it is commonly accepted, created this world. Therefore, I believe it is safe to presume that God also made that part of the world called Louisiana.

"Therefore, God, would be the owner of origin and His origins date back, to before the beginning of time, the world as we know it and the FHA.

"I hope you find God's original claim to be satisfactory. Now, may we have our damn loan?"

The loan was indeed approved.

THE LATE LARRY LAPRISE

With all the sadness and trauma going on in the world at the moment, it is worth reflecting on the death of a very important person which almost went unnoticed last week.

Larry LaPrise, the man who wrote "The Hokey Pokey," died peacefully at the age of 93. The most traumatic part for his family was getting him into the coffin.

They put his left leg in, and then the trouble started.

FRIENDS VS ITALIAN FRIENDS

Friends: Move out when they're 18 with the full support of their parents.
Italian Friends: Move out when they're 28, having saved for that nice house and are a week away from getting married...unless there's room in the basement for the newlyweds.

Friends: When their mom visits them she brings a nice bunt cake and you sip coffee and chat.
Italian Friends: When their mom visits them she brings 3 days worth of food and begins to immediately tidy up, dust, do the laundry, or rearrange the furniture.

Friends: Their dads always call before they come over to visit them and it's usually only on special occasions.
Italian Friends: Are not at all fazed when their dads come over, unannounced, on a Saturday morning at 8:00 am and start pruning the trees with a chainsaw or renovating the garage.

Friends: You can leave your kids with them and you always worry if everything is going to be OK, plus you have to feed them after you pick them up.
Italian Friends: No problem, leave the kids there and if they get out of line the Italian friend can set them straight...plus they get fed.

Friends: Always pay retail and look in the yellow pages when they need something done.
Italian Friends: Just call their dad or uncle and ask for another dad's or uncle's phone number to get it done...cash deal, knowwhatImean!

Friends: Will come over for cake and coffee and expect cake and coffee, no more.

Italian Friends: Will come over for cake and coffee and expect an antipasto, a few bottles of wine, a pasta dish, a choice of two meats, salad, bread, potatoes, a nice dessert cake, fruit, coffee and a few after dinner drinks…time permitting there will be a late dinner as well.

Friends: Think that being Italian is a great thing.
Italian Friends: Know that being Italian is a great thing.

Friends: Never ask for food.
Italian Friends: Are the reason you have no food.

Friends: Will say "hello."
Italian Friends: Will give you a big hug and a kiss.

Friends: Call your parents Mr. and Mrs.
Italian Friends: Call your parents mom and dad.

Friends: Have never seen you cry.
Italian Friends: Cry with you.

Friends: Will eat at your dinner table and leave.
Italian Friends: Will spend hours there, talking, laughing and just being together.

Friends: Borrow your stuff for a few days, then give it back.
Italian Friends: Keep your stuff so long they forget it's yours.

Friends: Know a few things about you.
Italian Friends: Could write a book with direct quotes from you.

Friends: Will leave you behind if that's what the crowd is doing.
Italian Friends: Will kick the whole crowds' ass that left you behind.

Friends: Would knock on your door.
Italian Friends: Walk right in and say, "I'm home!"

Friends: Are for a while.
Italian Friends: Are for life.

Friends: Will ignore this.
Italian Friends: Will forward this.

GOLF GOSPEL

1. Eighteen holes of match play will teach you more about your foe than 18 years of dealing with him across a desk. Grantland Rice.

2. Golf appeals to the idiot in us and the child. Just how childlike golf players become is proven by their frequent inability to count past five. John Updike.

3. It is almost impossible to remember how tragic a place the world is when on is playing golf. Robert Lynd.

4. If profanity had any influence on the flight of the ball, the game of golf would be played far better than it is. Horace G. Hutchinson.

5. They say golf is like life, but don't believe them. Gold is more complicated than that. Gardner Dickinson.

6. If a lot of people gripped a knife and fork as poorly as they do a gold club, they'd starve to death. Sam Snead.

7. Golf is a day spent in a round of strenuous idleness. William Wordsworth.

8. If you drink, don't drive. Don't even putt. Dean Martin.

9. If you are going to throw a club, it is important to throw it ahead of you, down the fairway, so you don't have to waste time and energy going back to pick it up. Tommy Bolt.

10. Man blames fate for all other accidents, but feels personally responsible when he makes a hole-in-one. Bishop Sheen.

11. I don't say my golf game is bad, but if I grew tomatoes they'd come up sliced. Arnold Palmer.

12. My handicap? Woods and irons. Chris Codirole.

13. The ardent golfer would play Mount Everest if somebody would put a flag stick on top. Pete Dye.

14. I'm hitting the woods just great; but having a terrible time getting out of them! Buddy Hackett.

15. The only time my prayers are never answered is playing golf. Billy Graham.

16. If you think it's hard to meet new people, try picking up the wrong golf ball. Jack Lemmon.

17. It's good sportsmanship to not pick up lost golf balls while they are still rolling. Mark Twain.

18. Don't play too much golf. Two rounds a day are plenty. Harry Vardon.

19. Golf and sex are the only things you can enjoy without being good at either of them. Jimmy DeMaret.

20. May thy ball lie in green pastures, and not in still waters. Ben Hogan.

21. If I hit it right, it's a slice. If I hit it left, it's a hook. If I hit it straight, it's a miracle. All Us Hackers.

22. The difference in golf and government is that in golf you can't improve your lie. George Deukmejian.

23. Golf is a game invented by the same people who think music comes out of a bagpipe. Lee Trevino.

24. Golf is a game you cannot win or lose. It is only a game you can play. Begger Vance.

A NEW VIRUS

There is a dangerous virus being passed around electronically, orally, and by hand. This virus is called Worm-Overload-Recreational-Killer (WORK). If you receive WORK from any of your colleagues, your boss, or anyone else via any means DO NOT TOUCH IT. This virus will wipe out your private life completely.

If you should come into contact with WORK, take two good friends to the nearest grocery store. Purchase the antidote known as Work-Isolating-Neutralizer-Extract (WINE) or Bothersome-Employer-Elimination-Rebooter (BEER). Take the antidote repeatedly until WORK has been completely eliminated from your system.
You should forward this warning to 5 friends. If you do not have 5 friends, you have already been infected and WORK is controlling your life.

INVESTMENT WISDOM

For all of you with any money left, be aware of the next expected mergers so that you can get in on the ground floor and make some Big Bucks. Watch for these mergers in 2007:

- Hale business Systems, Mary Kay Cosmetics, Filler Brush, and E.R. Grace Co. will merge and become: Hale, Mary, Filler, Grace.

- Polygram Records, Warner Bros., and Zesta Crackers join forces and become: Poly, Warner Cracker.

- 3M will merge with Goodyear and become: MMMGood.

- Zippo Manufacturing, Audi Motors, Dofasco, and Dakota Mining will merge and become: ZipAudiDoDa.

- FedEx is expected to join its major competitor, UPS and will become: FedUP.

- Fairchild Electronics and Honeywell Computers will become: Fairwell Honeychild.

- Grey Poupon and Docker Pants are expected to become: Poupon Pants.

- Knotts Berry Farm and the National Organization of Women will become: Knott NOW!

- Victoria's Secret and Smith & Wesson will merge under the new name: Titty Titty, Bang Bang!

221

PET DIARY

Excerpts from a Dog's Diary:

9:30 am - A car ride! My favorite thing!

9:40 am - A walk in the park! My favorite thing!

10:30 am - Got rubbed and petted! My favorite thing!

12:00 pm - Lunch! My favorite thing!

1:00 pm - Played in the yard! My favorite thing!

3:00 pm - Wagged my tail! My favorite thing!

5:00 pm - Milk bones! My favorite thing!

7:00 pm - Got to play ball! My favorite thing!

8:00 pm - Wow! Watched TV with the people! My favorite thing!

11:00 pm - Sleeping on the bed! My favorite thing!

Excerpts from a Cat's Diary

Day 983 of my captivity.

My captors continue to taunt me with bizarre little dangling objects. They dine lavishly on fresh meat, while the other inmates and I are fed hash or some sort of dry nuggets. Although I make my contempt for the rations perfectly clear, I nevertheless must eat something in order to keep up my strength. The only thing that keeps me going is my dream of escape. In an attempt to disgust them, I one again vomit on the carpet.

Today I decapitated a mouse and dropped its headless body at their feet. I had hoped this would strike fear into their hearts, since it clearly demonstrates what I am capable of. However, they merely made condescending comments about what a "good little hunter" I am. Bastards!

There was some sort of assembly of their accomplices tonight. I was placed in solitary confinement for the duration of the event. However, I could hear the noises and smell of food. I overheard that my confinement was due to the power of "allergies." I must learn what this means, and how to use it to my advantage. Today I was almost successful in an attempt to assassinate one of my tormentors by weaving around his feet as he was walking. I must try this again tomorrow – but at the top of the stairs.

I am convinced that the other prisoners here are flunkies and snitches. The dog receives special privileges. He is regularly released – and seems to be more than willing to return. He is obviously retarded. The bird has got to be an informant. I observed him communicate with the guards regularly. I am certain that he reports my every move. My captors have arranged protective custody for him in an elevated cell, so he is safe…for now.

NEW WORDS FOR 2007

Essential vocabulary additions for the workplace (and elsewhere)!

1. BLAMESTORMING: Sitting around in a group, discussing why a deadline was missed or a project failed, and who was responsible.

2. SEAGULL MANAGER: A manager, who flies in, makes a lot of noise, craps on everything, and then leaves.

3. ASSMOSIS: The process by which some people seem to absorb success and advancement by kissing up to the boss rather than working hard.

4. SALMON DAY: The experience of spending an entire day swimming upstream only to get screwed and die in the end.

5. CUBE FARM: An office filled with cubicles.

6. PRAIRIE DOGGIE: When someone yells or drops something loudly in a cube farm, and people's heads pop up over the walls to see what's going on.

7. MOUSE POTATO: The on-line, wired generation's answer to the couch potato.

8. SITCOMs: Single Income, Two Children, Oppressive Mortgage, What Yuppies get into when they have children and one of them stops working to say home with the kids.

9. STRESS PUPPY: A person who seems to thrive on being stressed out and whiny.

10. SWIPEOUT: An ATM or credit card that has been rendered useless because magnetic strip is worn away from extensive use.

11. ZEROX SUBSIDY: Euphemism for swiping free photocopies from one's workplace.

12. IRRITAINMENT: Entertainment and media spectacles that are annoying buy you find yourself unable to stop watching them.

13. PRECUSSIVE MAINTENANCE: The fine art of whacking the crap out of an electronic device to get it to work again. Often feel like doing this to my computer...

14. ADMINISPHERE: The rarefied organizational layers beginning just above the rand and file. Decisions that fall from the adminisphere are often profoundly inappropriate or irrelevant to the problems they were designed to solve.

15. 404: Someone who clueless. From the World Wide Web error Message "404 Not Found," meaning that the requested site could not be located.

16. GENERICA: Features of the American landscape that are exactly the same no matter where one is, such as fast food joints, strip malls, and subdivisions.

17. OHNOSECOND: That minuscule fraction of time in which you realize that you've just made a BIG mistake. (Like after hitting send on an email by mistake.)

18. WOOFS: Well-Off Older Folks.

19. CROP DUSTING: Surreptitiously passing gas while passing through a Cube Farm.

A GOOD MORTICIAN

A man who just died was delivered to the mortuary wearing an expensive, expertly tailored black suit. The mortician asks the deceased's wife how she would like the body dressed. He points out that the man does look good in the black suit he is already wearing.

The widow, however, says that she always thought her husband looked his best in blue, and that she wants him in a blue suit. She gives the mortician a blank check and says, "I don't care what it costs, but please have my husband in a blue suit for viewing."

The woman returns the next day for the wake. To her delight she finds her husband dressed in a gorgeous blue suit with a subtle chalk stripe; the suits fits him perfectly.

She says to the mortician, "Whatever this cost, I'm very satisfied. You did an excellent job and I'm very grateful. How much did you have to spend?"

To her astonishment, the mortician presents her with the blank check. "There's no charge," he says.

"No, really, I must compensate you for the cost of that exquisite blue suit!" she says.

"Honestly, ma'am," the mortician says, "it cost nothing. You see, a deceased gentlemen of about your husband's size was brought in shortly after you left yesterday and was wearing an attractive blue suit. I asked his wife if she minded him going to his grave wearing a black suit instead, and she said it made no difference as long as he looked nice. "So, I switched the heaps."

MENOPAUSE JEWELRY

My husband, being unhappy with my mood swings, bought me a mood ring the other day so he would be able to monitor my moods.

We've discovered that when I'm in a good mood, it turns green. When I'm in a bad mood, it leaves a big f - - red mark on his forehead. Maybe next time he'll buy me a diamond.

USRSF

The Pentagon announced today the formation of a new 500-man elite fighting unit called the United States Redneck Special Forces (USRSF)...

These Alabama, Arkansas, Georgia, Kentucky, Mississippi, West Virginia, Missouri, Oklahoma, Tennessee, and Texas boys will be dropped off into Iraq and have been given only the following facts about terrorists:

1. The season opens today.

2. There is no limit.

3. They taste just like chicken.

4. They don't like beer, pickups, country music or Jesus.

5. They are directly responsible for the death of Dale Earnhardt.

The Pentagon expects the problem in Iraq to be over by Friday.

LAST CHILD SUPPORT CHECK

Today be my baby girls 18th birthday. I be so glad that dis be my last child support payment. Month after month, year after year, all dose payments. So I call my baby girl, LaKeesha, to come to my house, and when she get here, I say, "Baby girl, I want you to take dis check over to you momma house and tell her dis be the last check she ever getting' from me, and I want you to come back and tell me the 'spression on you momma's face."

So, my baby girl take the check over to her momma. I be anxious to hear what she say, and bout the 'sspression on her face. Baby girl walk through the door, I say, "Now what yo momma say 'bout that?" She say to tell you that "you ain't my daddy, and watch the 'spression on yo face!!!"

THE GOOD OLD DAYS

Scenario: Jack pulls into school parking lot with rifle in gun rack.

1956 -Vice President comes over, takes a look at Jack's rifle, goes to his car and gets his to show Jack.
2006 – School goes into lockdown, FBI called, Jack hauled off to fail and never sees his truck or gun again. Counselors called in for traumatized students and teachers.

Scenario: Johnny and Mark get into a fist fight after school.

1956 – Crowd gathers, Mark wins. Johnny and Mark shake hands and end up best friends. Nobody goes to jail, nobody arrested, nobody expelled.
2006 – Police called, SWAT team arrives, arrests Johnny and Mark. Charged them with assault, both expelled even though Johnny started it.

Scenario: Jeffery won't be still in class, disrupts other students.

1956 – Jeffery sent to office and given a good paddling by Principal. Sits still in class.
2006 – Jeffery given huge doses of Ritalin. Becomes a zombie. School gets extra money from state because Jeffery has a disability.

Scenario: Billy breaks a window in his father's car and his Dad gives him a whipping.

1956 – Billy is more careful next time, grows up normal, goes to college, and becomes a successful businessman.

2006 – Billy's Dad is arrested for child abuse. Billy removed to foster care and joins a gang. Billy's sister is told by state psychologist that she remembers being abused herself and their Dad goes to prison. Billy's mom has affair with psychologist.

Scenario: Mark gets a headache and takes some headache medicine to school.

1956 – Mark shares headache medicine with Principal out on the smoking dock.

2006 - Police called, Mark expelled from school for drug violations. Car searched for drugs and weapons.

Scenario: Mary turns up pregnant.

1973 – Five High School Boys leave town. Mary does her senior year at a special school for expectant mothers.

2006: - Middle School Counselor calls Planned Parenthood, who notifies the ACLU. Mary is driven to the next state over and gets an abortion without her parent's consent or knowledge. Mary given condoms and told to be more careful next time.

Scenario: Pedro fails high school English.

1973 – Pedro goes to summer school, passes English, goes to college.

2006 – Pedro's cause is taken up. Newspaper articles appear nationally explaining that teaching English as a requirement for graduation is racist. ACLU files class action lawsuit against state school system and Pedro's English teacher. English banned from core curriculum. Pedro given diploma anyway, but ends up moving lawns for a living because he can't speak English.

Scenario: Johnny takes apart leftover firecrackers from the 4th of July, puts them in a model airplane paint bottle, blows up a red ant bed.

1956 – Ants die.

2006 – BATF, Homeland Security, FBI called. Johnny charged with domestic terrorism, FBI investigates parents, siblings removed from home, computers confiscated, Johnny's dad goes on a terror watch list and is never allowed to fly again.

Scenario: Johnny falls while running during recess and scrapes his knee. He is found crying by his teacher, Mary. Mary, hugs him to comfort him.

1956 – In a short time Johnny feels better and goes on playing.

2006 – Mary is accused of being a sexual predator and loses her job. She faces 3 years in State Prison.

2008

TWO COWS

You have two cows. You sell one and buy a bull. Your herd multiplies, and the economy grows. You sell them and retire on the income.

AN AMERICAN CORPORATION
You have two cows. You sell one, and force the other to produce the milk of four cows. You are surprised when the cow drops dead.

ENRON VENTURE CAPITALISM
You have two cows. You sell three of them to your publicly listed company, using letters of credit opened by your brother-in-law at the bank, then execute a debt/equity swap with an associated general offer so that you get all four cows back, with a tax exemption for five cows. The milk rights of the six cows are transferred via an intermediary to a Cayman Island company secretly owned by the majority shareholder who sells the rights to all seven cows back to your listed company. The annual report says the company owns eight cows, with an option on one more. Sell one cow to buy a new president of the United States, leaving you with nine cows. No balance sheet provided with the release. The public buys your bull.

ARTHUR ANDERSON, LLC
You have two cows. You shred all documents that Enron has any cows, take two cows from Enron for payment for consulting the cows, and attest that Enron has 9 cows.

A FRENCH CORPORATION
You have two cows. You go on strike because you want three cows.

A JAPANESE CORPORATION
You have two cows. You redesign them so they are one-tenth the size of an ordinary cow and produce twenty times the milk. You then create clever cow cartoon images called Cowkimon and market them World-Wide.

A GERMAN CORPORATION
You have two cows. You reengineer them so they live for 200 years, eat once a month, and milk themselves.

A BRITISH CORPORATION
You have two cows. Both are mad.

AN ITALIAN CORPORATION
You have two cows, but you don't know where they are. You break for lunch.

A RUSSIAN CORPORATION
You have two cows. You count them and learn you have five cows. You count them again and learn you have 42 cows. You count them again and learn you have 12 cows. You stop counting cows and open another bottle of vodka.

A SWISS CORPORATION
You have 500 cows, none of which belong to you. You charge others for storing them.

A HINDU CORPORATION
You have two cows. You worship them.

A CHINESE CORPORATION

You have two cows. You have 300 people milking them. You claim full employment, high bovine productivity, and attest the newsman who reported the numbers.

AN ISRAELI CORPORATION
So, there are these two Jewish cows, right? They open a milk factory, and ice cream store, and then sell the movie rights. They send their calves to Harvard to become doctors. So, who needs people?

AN ARKANSAS CORPORATION
You have two cows. That one on the left is kinda cute....

GETTING' OLD

Three sisters ages 92, 94 and 96 live in a house together. One night the 96 year old draws a bath. She puts her foot in and pauses. She yells to the other sisters, "Was I getting in or out of the bath?"

The 94 year old yells back, "I don't know. I'll come up and see." She starts up the stairs and pauses. "Was I going up the stairs or down?"

The 92 year old is sitting at the kitchen table having tea listening to her sisters. She shakes her head and says, "I sure hope I never get that forgetful."

She knocks on wood for good measure. She yells, "I'll come up and help both of you as soon as I see who's at the door."

GOLF

Golf can best be defined as an endless series of tragedies obscured by the occasional miracle, followed by a good bottle of beer.

Golf! You hit down to make the ball go up. You swing left and the ball goes right. The lowest score wins. And on top of that, the winner buys the drinks!

Golf is harder than baseball. In golf, you have to play your foul balls.

If you find you do not mind playing golf in the rain, the snow, even during a hurricane, here's a valuable tip: your life is in trouble.

Golfers, who try to make everything perfect, before taking the shot, rarely make a perfect shot.

The term 'mulligan' is really a contraction of the phrase "mul it again.'

A 'gimme' can best be defined as an arrangement between two golfers, neither of whom can putt very well.

An interesting thing about golf is that no matter how badly you play, it is always possible to get worse.

Golf's a hard game to figure. One day you'll go out and slice it and shank it, hit into all the traps and miss every green. The next day you go out and for no reason at all you really stink.

If your best shots are the practice swing and the 'gimme putt,' you might wish to reconsider this game.

Golf is the only sport where the most feared opponent is you.

Golf is like marriage: If you take yourself too seriously it won't work and both are expensive.

The best wood in most amateur's bags is the pencil.

DAVE LETTERMAN'S TOP TEN REASONS WHY GOLF IS BETTER THAN SEX

10. A below par performance is considered darn good.

9. You can stop in the middle and have a cheeseburger and couple of beers.

8. It's much easier to find the sweet spot.

7. Foursomes are encouraged.

6. You can still make money doing it as a senior.

5. Three times a day is possible.

4. Your partner doesn't hire a lawyer if you play with someone else.

3. If you live in Florida, you can do it almost every day.

2. You don't have to cuddle with your partner when you're finished.

1. When your equipment gets old you can replace it!

THE FLORIDA CODE

When giving directions to Florida, you should always start with the words, 'take I-75, I-4 or take I-95.'

If you're a snowbird or a non-working retiree, you absolutely cannot drive between the hours of 6am and 10am and 4pm and 7pm. This is considered to be rush hour and you're not in any rush. No exceptions.

Freeways can only go north and south. Not east and west. Tolls are a fact of life down here, the state has to make money so deal with it! Interstates will always be under construction … that's the law, there is nothing anyone can do about it, period.

A1A and Alt A1A are the same streets.

Traffic lights aren't timed and never will be.

We measure the distance you travel in time, not miles.

If you travel more than 5 – 10 miles on any road in any part of Florida without seeing an orange 'Bob's Barricade," you're lost!

If you miss your exit on I-75, I-4, I-95, or I-275, it's perfectly acceptable to back up. Every street in Florida has both a name and a number (i.e. In Tampa there is Adamo – 60th) just for the heck of it and for the pleasure we get from the reaction of visitors when we give them directions.

Once the light turns green, only 3 cars can go through the intersection. Eight more go through on yellow, and 4 on red.

Know the difference between Sun Pass, Sun Fest, Sun-Sentinel, and Sun Trust.

Flip flops, tank tops and baggy shorts are also known as business casual.

Your blinker means nothing.

English is our first and second language.

It is perfectly acceptable to brag about the size of your generator.

We have alligators here in Florida and they WILL bite you. Don't be stupid and try to feed or pet one.

When a hurricane is headed our way, even though you have advanced warning and you are told to be prepared, you're not a true Floridian unless you wait until the absolute last minute to go to Home Depot to pick up plywood or to Publix to stock up water, ice, beer, and potato chips.

You know how to spell Okeechobee. There is an Okeechobee Blvd, Street, Avenue, Town, Lake and County.

A true Floridian does NOT own a boat. They make friends with someone who already owns one. That way you don't have to deal with any of the headaches.

You weren't born here. If you were, you're angry that everyone else moved here.

There's always a Walgreens across the street from a CVS on almost every corner – with more being built every day.

When picking up a woman on South Beach, always look for an Adams apple.

It's normal to sweat when you are putting up your holiday decorations.

Jupiter is a city, not a planet.

Seniors have to do their errands during the weekdays. Not weeknights or weekends – that's for the forking folks.

There are three types of dolphins, Mahi-mahi, Flipper, and also one called a football team.

You can't say; 'this is how we did it up north.' If you think that way, then go back.

No matter what they decide in Tallahassee you will never, ever be able to figure out your property taxes.

Learn how to dress in layers. It will be 95 degrees outside, but inside any restaurant or business it's 65 degrees.

There are three things you will need to survive a Florida winter: A long sleeved T-shirt, sunscreen and the ability to mock all those extremely pale 'visitors' with the bright pink 'Florida tans.'

The same neighbor who smiles at you every day will be the first one to rat you out if you are violating water restrictions.

THE FROG AND GOLF

A man takes the day off work and decides to go out golfing. He is on the second hole when he notices a grog sitting next to the green. He thinks nothing of it and is about to shoot when he hears, "Ribbit 9 Iron." The man looks around and doesn't see anyone. Again, he hears, "Ribbit 9 Iron." He looks at the frog and decides to prove the frog wrong. He puts the club away, and grabs an 8 iron.

BOOM! He hits it 10 inches from the cup. He is shocked. He says to the frog, "Wow that's amazing. You must be a lucky frog, eh?"

The man decides to take the frog with him to the next hole. "What do you think frog?" the man asks. "Ribbit 3 wood." The guy takes out a 3 wood and, BOOM. Hole in one.

The man is befuddled and doesn't know what to say. By the end of the day, the man golfed the best game of golf in his life and asks the frog, "OK, where to next?" The frog replies, "Ribbit Las Vegas."

They go to Las Vegas and the guy says, "OK frog, now what?" The frog says, "Ribbit Roulette." Upon approaching the roulette table, the man asks, "What do you think I should bet?" The frog replies, "Ribbit $3000, black 6."

Now, this is a million-to-one shot to win, but after the golf game the man figures what the heck. BOOM! Tons of cash comes sliding back across the table. The man takes his winnings and buys the best room in the hotel. He sits the frog down and says, "Frog, I don't know how to repay you. You've won me all this money and I am forever grateful."

The frog replies, "Ribbit Kiss Me." He figures why not, since after all the frog did for him, he deserves it. With a kiss, the frog turns into a gorgeous 15-year old girl. "And that, your honor, is how the girl ended up in my room. So help me God, or my name is not William Jefferson Clinton."

PRISON AND WORK

Just in case you ever get these two environments mixed up, this comparison should make things a little more clear.

Prison: You spend most of your time in a 10X10 cell
Work: You spend most of your time in a 6X6 cubicle

Prison: You get three fully paid for meals a day
Work: You get a break for one meal, and you have to pay for it

Prison: For good behavior, you get time off
Work: For good behavior, you get more work

Prison: The guard locks and unlocks all the doors for you
Work: You must carry a security card and open all the doors yourself

Prison: You can watch TV and play games
Work: You could get fired for watching TV and playing games

Prison: You get your own toilet
Work: You have to share the toilet with people who pee on the seat

Prison: They allow your family and friends to visit
Work: You aren't even supposed to speak to your family

Prison: All expenses are paid by the taxpayers with no work required on your part
Work: You must pay all your expenses to go to work, and they deduct taxes from your salary to pay for prisoners

Prison: You spend most of your life inside bars wanting to get out

Work: You spend most of your time wanting to get out and go inside bars

Prison: You must deal with sadistic wardens
Work: They are called 'managers'

There is something seriously wrong with this picture.

WHY AM I MARRIED?

- You have two choices in life: You can stay single and be miserable, or get married and wish you were dead.

- At a cocktail party, one woman said to another, "Aren't you wearing your wedding ring on the wrong finger?" "Yes, I am. I married the wrong man."

- A lady inserted an ad in the classifieds: "Husband Wanted." Next day she received a hundred letters. They all said the same thing: "You can have mine."

- When a woman steals your husband, there is no better revenge than to let her keep him.

- A woman is incomplete until she is married. Then she is finished.

- A little boy asked his father, "Daddy, how much does it cost to get married." Father replied, "I don't know son, I'm still paying."

- A young son asked, "Is it true Dad that in some parts of Africa a man doesn't know his wife until he marries her?" Dad replied, "That happens in every country, son."

- Then there was a woman who said, "I never knew what real happiness was until I got married, and by then, it was too late."

- Marriage is the triumph of imagination over intelligence.

- If you want your spouse to listen and pay strict attention to every word you say…talk in your sleep.

- Just think, if it weren't for marriage, men would go through life thinking they had no faults at all.

- First guy says, "My wife's an angel!" Second guy remarks, "You're lucky, mine's still alive."

- "A Woman's Prayer: Dear Lord, I pray for: Wisdom to understand a man, to Love and to forgive him, and for Patience for his moods. Because Lord, if I pray for Strength I'll just beat him to death."

AND FOR THE FAVORITE!!

- Husband and wife are waiting at the bus stop with their nine children. A blind man joins them after a few minutes. When the bus arrives, they find it overloaded and only the wife and the nine kids are able to fit onto the bus. So the husband and the blind man decide to walk. After a while, the husband gets irritated by the ticking of the stick of the blind man as he taps it on the sidewalk, and says to him, "Why don't you put a piece of rubber at the end of your stick? That ticking sound is driving me crazy." The blind man replies, "If you had put a rubber at the end of your stick, we'd be riding the bus, so shut the hell up."

SURGERY

Five surgeons from big cities are discussing who makes the best patients to operate on.

The first surgeon, from New York, says, "I like to see accountants on my operating table, because when you open them up, everything inside is numbered."

The second, from Chicago, responds, "Yeah, but you should try electricians! Everything inside them is color coded."

The third surgeon, from Dallas, says, "No, I really think librarians are the best, everything inside them is in alphabetical order."

The fourth surgeon, from Los Angeles chimes in: "You know, I like construction workers...those guys always understand when you have a few parts left over."

But the fifth surgeon, from Washington, DC shut them all up when he observed: "You're all wrong. Politicians are the easiest to operate on. There's no guts, no heart, no balls, no brains and no spine, and the head and the ass are interchangeable."

SOME PHILOSOPHY FOR THE WEEKEND

A newlywed couple had only been married for two weeks. The husband, although very much in love, couldn't wait to go out on the town and party with his old buddies.

So, he said to his new wife, 'Honey, I'll be right back.'

'Where are you going, coochy cooh.' asked the wife.

'I'm going to the bar, pretty face. I'm going to have a beer.'

The wife said, 'You want a beer, my love?'

She opened the door to the refrigerator and showed him 25 different kinds of beer brands from 12 different countries: Germany, Holland, Japan, India, etc.

The husband didn't know what to do, and the only thing that he could think of saying was, 'Yes, lolly pop … but at the bar … you know … they have frozen glasses…'

He didn't get to finish the sentence, because the wife interrupted him by saying, 'You want a frozen glass, puppy face.'

She took a huge beer mug out of the freezer, so frozen that she was getting chills just holding it.

The husband, looking a bit pale, said, 'Yes, tootsie roll, but at the Bar they have those hors d'oeuvres that are really delicious…I won't be long, I'll be right back. I promise. OK?'

'You want hors d'oeuvres, poochi pooh?' She opened the oven and took out 5 dishes of different hors d'oeuvres: chicken wings, pigs in a blanket, mushroom caps, pork strips, etc.

"But my sweet honey...At the bar...You know...there's swearing, dirty words and all that....'

'You want dirty words, Dickhead." Drink your fu***ing beer in your Goddamn frozen mug and eat your motherf***ing snacks, because you are Married now, and you aren't f***ing going anywhere! Got it, Asshole?'

...And, they lived happily ever after.

BABY'S FIRST EXAMINATION

A woman and a baby were in the doctor's examining room, waiting for the doctor to come in for the baby's first exam.

The doctor arrived, and examined the baby, checked his weight, and being a Little concerned, asked if the baby was breast-fed or bottle fed? 'Breast fed,' she replied.

'Well, strip down to your waist,' the doctor ordered. She did. He pinched her nipples, pressed, kneaded, and rubbed both breasts for a while in a very professional and detailed examination. Motioning to her to get dressed, the doctor said, 'No wonder this baby is underweight. You don't have any milk.'

'I know,' she said, 'I'm his Grandma, but I'm glad I came.'

ROBOT LIE DETECTOR

John was a salesman's delight when it came to any kind of unusual gimmick. His wife Marsha had long ago given up trying to get him to change. One day John came home with another one of his unusual purchases. It was a robot that John claimed was actually a lie detector.

It was about 5:30 that afternoon when Tommy, their 11 year old son, returned home from school. Tommy was over 2 hours late.

"Where have you been? Why are you over 2 hours late getting home?" asked John.

"Several of us went to the library to work on an extra credit project," said Tommy.

The robot then walked around the table and slapped Tommy, knocking him completely out of his chair.

"Son," said John, "this robot is a lie detector. Now tell us where you really were after school."

"We went to Bobby's house and watched a movie." said Tommy.

"What did you watch?" asked Marsha.

"The Ten Commandments." answered Tommy.

The robot went around to Tommy and once again slapped him, knocking him off his chair once more.

With his lip quivering, Tommy got up, sat down and said, "I am sorry I lied. We really watched a tape called Sex Queen."

"I am ashamed of you son," said John. "When I was your age, I never lied to my parents."

The robot then walked around to John and delivered a whack that nearly knocked him out of his chair.

Marsha doubled over in laughter, almost in tears and said, "Boy, did you ever ask for that one! You can't be too mad with Tommy. After all, he is your son!"

With that the robot immediately walked around to Marsha and slapped her right off her chair.

RIGHT ON, ANDY ROONEY

I don't think being a minority makes you a victim of anything except numbers. The only things I can think of that are truly discriminatory are things like the United Negro College Fund, Jet Magazine, Black Entertainment Television, and Miss Black America.

Try to have things like the United Caucasian College Fund, Cloud Magazine, White Entertainment Television, or Miss White America; and see what happens...Jesse Jackson will be knocking down your door.

Guns do not make you a killer. I think killing makes you a killer. You can kill someone with a baseball bat or a car, but no one is trying to ban you from driving to the ball game.

I believe they are called the Boy Scouts for a reason, which is why there are no girls allowed. Girls belong in the Girl Scouts! Are you listening Martha Burke?

I think if you feel homosexuality is wrong, it is not a phobia, it is an opinion.

I have the right 'NOT' to be tolerant of others because they are different, weird, or tick me off.

When 70% of the people who get arrested are black, in cities where 70% of the population is black, that is not racial profiling; it is the Law of Probability.

I believe that if you are selling me a milkshake, a pack of cigarettes, a newspaper or a hotel room, you must do it in English! As a matter of fact, if you want to be an American citizen, you should have to speak English!

My father and grandfather didn't die in vain so you can leave the countries you were born in to come over here and disrespect ours.

I think the police should have every right to shoot you if you threaten them after they tell you to stop. If you can't understand the word 'freeze' or 'stop' in English, see the above lines.

I don't think just because you were born in this country, you are qualified for any special loan programs, government sponsored bank loans or tax breaks, etc, so you can open a hotel, coffee shop, trinket store, or any other business.

We did not go to the aid of certain foreign countries and risk our lives in wars to defend their freedoms, so that decades later they could come over here and tell us our constitution is a living document; and open to their interpretations.

I don't hate the rich and I don't pity the poor.

I know pro wrestling is fake, but so are movies and television. That doesn't stop you from watching them.

I think Bill Gates has every right to keep every penny he made and continue to make more. If it ticks you off, go and invent the next operating system that's better, and put your name on the building.

It doesn't take a whole village to raise a child right, but it does take a parent to stand up to the kid; and smack their little behinds when necessary, and say 'NO!'

I think tattoos and piercing are fine if you want them, but please don't pretend they are a political statement. And, please, stay home until that new lip ring heals. I don't want to look at your ugly infected mouth as you serve me French fries!

I am sick of 'Political Correctness.' I know a lot of black people, and not a single one of them was born in Africa; so how can they be 'African-Americans'? Besides, Africa is a continent. I don't go around saying I am a European-American because my great, great, great, great, great grandfather was from Europe. I am proud to be from America and nowhere else.

And if you don't like my point of view, tough....

PLEDGE OF ALLEGIANCE

I pledge allegiance to the flag, of the United States of America, and to the Republic for which it stands, one Nation under God, indivisible, with Liberty and Justice for All!

It is said that 86% of Americans believe in God. Therefore I have a very hard time understanding why there is such a problem in having 'In God We Trust' on our money and having 'God' in the Pledge of Allegiance. Why don't we just tell the 14% to BE QUIET!!!

JUST A LITTLE REST

An older, tired-looking dog wandered into my yard; I could tell from his collar and well-fed belly that he had a home and was well taken care of.

He calmly came over to me, I gave him a few pats on the head; he then followed me into my house, slowly walked down the hall, curled up in the corner and fell asleep. An hour later, he went to the door, and I let him out.

The next day he was back, greeted me in my yard, walked inside and resumed his spot in the hall and again slept for about an hour. This continued off and on for several weeks.

Curious, I pinned a note to his collar: "I would like to find out who the owner of this wonderful sweet dog is and ask if you are aware that almost every afternoon your dog comes to my house for a nap."

The next day he arrived for his nap, with a different note pinned to his collar: "He lives in a home with 6 children, 2 under the age of 3 – he's trying to catch up on his sleep. Can I come with him tomorrow?"

HELICOPTER RIDE

Paul and his wife Mary went to the state fair every year, and every year Paul would say, "Mary, I'd like to ride in that helicopter." Mary always replied, "I know Paul, but that helicopter ride is fifty dollars, and fifty dollars is fifty dollars."

One year Paul and Mary went to the fair, and Paul said, Mary, "I'm 85 years old. If I don't ride that helicopter, I might never get another chance." To this, Mary replied, "Paul, that helicopter ride is fifty dollars, and fifty dollars is fifty dollars."

The pilot overheard the couple and said, "Folks, I'll make you a deal. I'll take the both of you for a ride. If you can stay quiet for the entire ride and not say a word, I won't charge you! But if you say one word, it's fifty dollars."

Paul and Mary agreed and up they went. The pilot did all kinds of fancy maneuvers, but not a word was heard. He did his daredevil tricks over and over again, but still not a word.

When they landed, the pilot turned to Paul and said, "By golly, I did everything I could to get you to yell out, but you didn't. I'm impressed!"

Paul replied, "Well, to tell you the truth, I almost said something when Mary fell out, but you know, fifty dollars is fifty dollars!"

BRITAIN IS REPOSSESSING THE U.S.A.

A message from John Cleese to the citizens of the United States of America.

In light of your failure to nominate competent candidates for the next President of the USA, and thus to govern yourselves, we hereby give notice of the revocation of your independence, effective immediately.

Her Sovereign Majesty Queen Elizabeth II will resume monarchical duties over all states, commonwealths, and territories (except Kansas, which she does not fancy).

Your new Prime Minister, Gordon Brown, will appoint a Governor for America without the need for further elections. Congress and the Senate will be disbanded.

A questionnaire may be circulated next year to determine whether any of you noticed. To aid in the transition to a British Crown Dependency, the following rules are introduced with immediate effect. As preparation, you should look up 'revocation' in the Oxford English Dictionary.

1. Then look up aluminum, and check the pronunciation guide. You will be amazed at just how wrongly you have been pronouncing it.

2. The letter 'U' will be reinstated in words such as 'favour' and 'neighbour.' Likewise, you will learn to spell 'doughnut' without skipping half the letters, and the suffix- ize will be replaced by the suffix – ise. Generally, you will be expected to raise your vocabulary to acceptable.

3. Using the same twenty-seven words interspersed with filler noises such as 'like' and 'you know' is an unacceptable and inefficient form of communication. There is no such thing as US English. We will let Microsoft know on your behalf. The Microsoft spell-checker will be adjusted to take account of the reinstated letter 'u' and the elimination of –ize. You will relearn your original national anthem, God Save the Queen.

4. July 4th will no longer be celebrated as a holiday.

5. You will learn to resolve personal issues without using guns, lawyers, or therapists. The fact that you need so many lawyers and therapists shows that you're not adult enough to be independent. Guns should only be handled by adults. If you're not adult enough to sort things out without suing someone or speaking to a therapist, then you're not grown up enough to handle a gun.

6. Therefore, you will no longer be allowed to own or carry anything more dangerous than a vegetable peeler. A permit will be required if you wish to carry a vegetable peeler in public.

7. All American cars are hereby banned. They are crap and this is For Your Own Good. When we show you German cars, you will understand what we mean.

8. All intersections will be replaced with roundabouts, and you will start driving on the left with immediate effect and without the benefit of conversation tables. Both roundabouts and metrication will help you understand the British sense of humor.

9. The Former USA will adopt UK prices on petrol (which you have been calling gasoline) – roughly $6/US gallon. Get used to it.

10. You will learn to make real chips. Those things you call French fries are not real chips, and those things you insist on calling potato chips are properly called crisps. Real chips are

thick cut, fried in animal fat, and dressed not with catsup but with vinegar.

11. The cold tasteless stuff you insist on calling beer is not actually beer at all. Henceforth, only proper British Bitter will be referred to as beer, and European brews of known and accepted provenance will be referred to as Lager. South Africa beer is also acceptable as they are pound for pound the greatest sporting Nation on earth and it can only be due to the beer. They are also part British Commonwealth – see what it did for them.

12. Hollywood will be required occasionally to cast English actors as good guys. Hollywood will also be required to cast English actors to play English characters. Watching Andie McDowell attempt English dialogue in Four Weddings and a Funeral was an experience akin to having one's ears removed with a cheese grater.

13. You will cease playing American football. There is only one kind of proper football; you call it soccer. Those of you brave enough will, in time, be allowed to play rugby (which has some similarities to American football, but does not involve stopping for a rest every twenty seconds or wearing full Kevlar body armour like a bunch of nancies). Don't try Rugby, the South Africans and Kiwis will thrash you, like they regularly thrash us.

14. Further, you will stop playing baseball. It is not reasonable to host an event called the World Series for a game which is not played outside of America. Since only 2.1% of you are aware that there is a world beyond your borders, your error is understandable. You will learn cricket, and we will let you face the South Africans first to take the sting out of their deliveries.

15. You must tell us who killed JFK. It's been driving us mad.

16. An internal revenue agent (i.e. a tax collector) from Her Majesty's Government will be with you shortly to ensure the acquisition of all monies due (Backdated to 1776).

17. Daily Tea Time begins promptly at 4 PM with proper cups, never mugs, and brewed in a teapot, with high quality biscuits (cookies), and cakes; strawberries in season, of course.

God save the Queen. Only He can!

SUMMARY OF MY LAST YEAR ON THE COMPUTER

I must send my thanks to whoever sent me the one about rat poop in the glue on envelopes because I now have to use a wet towel with every envelope that needs sealing.

Also, now I have to scrub the top of every can I open for the same reason.

I no longer have any savings because I gave it to a sick girl (Penny Brown) who is about to die in the hospital for the 1,387,258th time.

I no longer have any money at all, but that will change once I receive the $15,000 that Bill Gates/Microsoft and AOL are sending me for participating in their special e-mail program.

I no longer worry about my soul because I have 363,214 angels looking out for me, and St. Thomas novena has granted my every wish.

I no longer fear KFC because their chickens are actually horrible mutant freaks with no eyes or feathers.

I no longer use cancer-causing deodorants even though I smell like a water buffalo on a hot day.

Thanks to you, I have learned that my prayers only get answered if I forward an email to seven of my best friends and make a wish within five minutes.

Because of your concern, I no longer drink Coca Cola because it can remove toilet stains.

I no longer can buy gasoline without taking a man along to watch the car so a serial killer won't crawl in my back seat when I'm pumping gas.

I no longer drink Pepsi or Dr. Pepper since the people who make these products are atheists who refuse to put "Under God" on their cans.

I no longer use Saran wrap in the microwave because it causes cancer.

And thanks for letting me know I can't boil a cup of water in the microwave anymore because it will blow up in my face…disfiguring me for life.

I no longer check the coin return on pay phones because I could be pricked with a needle infected with AIDS.

I no longer go to shopping malls because someone will drug me with a perfume sample and rob me.

I no longer receive packages from UPS or FedEx since they are actually Al Qaeda in disguise.

I no longer shop at Target since they are French and don't support our American Troops or the Salvation Army.

I no longer answer to phone because someone will ask me to dial a number for which I will get a phone bill with calls to Jamaica, Uganda, Singapore, and Uzbekistan.

I no longer have any sneakers – but that will change once I receive my free replacement pair from Nike.

I no longer buy expensive cookies from Neiman Marcus since I now have their recipe.

Thanks to you, I can't use anyone's toilet but mine because a big brown African spider is lurking under the seat to cause me instant death when it bites my butt.

Thank you too for all the endless advice Andy Rooney has given us. I can live a better life now because he's told us how to fix everything.

And thanks to your great advice, I can't ever pick up $5.00 I dropped in the parking lot because it probably was placed there by a sex molester waiting underneath my car to grab my leg.

Oh, and don't forget this one either! I can no longer drive my car because I can't buy gas from certain gas companies!

If you don't send this e-mail to at least 144,000 people in the next 70 minutes, a large dove with diarrhea will land on your head at 5:00 PM this afternoon and the fleas from 12 camels will infest your back, causing you to grow a hairy hump. I know this will occur because it actually happened to a friend of my next door neighbor's ex-mother-in-law's second husband's cousin's beautician....

Have a wonderful day...A South American scientist from Argentina, after a lengthy study, has discovered that people with insufficient brain activity read their e-mail with their hand on the mouse.

Don't bother taking it off now, it's too late.

WHY WE LOVE CHILDREN

A kindergarten pupil told his teacher he'd found a cat, but it was dead. "How do you know that the cat was dead?" she asked him. "Because I pissed in its ear and it didn't move," answered the child innocently. "You did WHAT!!" the teacher exclaimed in surprise. "You know," explained the boy. "I leaned over and went 'Psssst!' and it didn't move."

A little girl goes to the barber shop with her father. She stands next to the barber chair, while her dad gets his hair cut, eating a snack cake. The barber says to her, "Sweetheart, you're gonna get hair on your Twinkie." She says, "Yes, I know, and I'm gonna get boobs, too."

An exasperated mother, whose son was always getting into mischief, finally asked him, "How do you expect to get into Heaven?" The boy thought it over and said, "Well, I'll run in and out and in and out and keep slamming the door until St. Peter says, 'For Heaven's sake, Dylan, come in or stay out!'"

One summer evening during a violent thunderstorm a mother was tucking her son into bed. She was about to turn off the light when he asked with a tremor in his voice, "Mommy, will you sleep with me tonight?" The mother smiled and gave him a reassuring hug. "I can't dear," she said, "I have to sleep in Daddy' room." A long silence was broken at last by his shaky little voice. "The big sissy."

It was that time, during the Sunday morning service, for the children's sermon. All the children were invited to come forward. One little girl was wearing a particularly pretty dress and, as she sat down, the pastor leaned over and said, "That is a very pretty dress. Is it your

Easter Dress?" The little girl replied, directly into the pastor's clip-on microphone, "Yes, and my Mom says it's a bitch to iron."

When I was six months pregnant with my third child, my three year-old came into the room as I was preparing to get into the shower. She said, "Mommy, you are getting fat!" I replied, "Yes, honey, remember Mommy has a baby growing in her tummy." "I know," she replied, "but what's growing in your butt?"

One day the first grade teacher was reading the story of Chicken Little to her class. She came to the part where Chicken Little warns the farmer. She read, "…and Chicken Little went up to the farmer and said, 'The sky is falling!'" The teacher then asked the class, "And what do you think that farmer said?" One little girl raised her hand and said, "I think he said: 'Holy shit! A talking chicken!'" The teacher was unable to teach for the next 10 minutes.

THE PLAN!
by Robin Williams

You gotta love Robin Williams...even if he's nuts! Leave it to him to come up with the perfect plan. He says...(and it's hard to argue with this logic!)...

"I see a lot of people yelling for peace, but I have not heard of a plan for peace. So, here's one plan."

1. The U.S. will apologize to the world for our 'interference' in their affairs, past and present. You know, Hitler, Mussolini, Stalin, Tojo, Noriega, Milosevic, Hussein, and the rest of those 'good ol' boys,' we will never 'interfere' again.

2. We will withdraw our troops from all over the world, starting with Germany, South Korea, the Middle East, and the Philippines. They don't want us there. Instead we would station troops at our borders. No one would be allowed to sneak through holes in the fence.

3. All illegal aliens have 90 days to get their affairs together and leave. We'll give them a free trip home. After 90 days the remainder will be gathered up and deported immediately, regardless of whom or where they are. They're illegal!!! France will welcome them.

4. All future visitors will be thoroughly checked and limited to 90 days unless given a special permit!!! No one from a terrorist nation will be allowed in. If you don't like it there, change it yourself and don't hide here. Asylum would never be available to anyone. We don't need any more cab drivers or 7-11 cashiers.

5. No foreign 'students' will be allowed here over age 21. The older ones are the bombers. If the students don't attend classes, they get a 'D' and it's back home, baby.

6. The U.S. will make a strong effort to become self-sufficient energy wise. This will include developing nonpolluting sources of energy but will require a temporary drilling of oil in the Alaskan wilderness. The caribou will have to cope for a while.

7. Offer Saudi Arabia and other oil producing countries $10 a barrel for their oil. If they don't like it, we go somewhere else. They can go somewhere else to sell their oil production. (About a week of wells filling up all the storage sites should be enough.)

8. If there is a famine or other natural catastrophe in the world, we will now 'interfere.' They can pray to Allah or whomever for seeds, rain, cement or whatever else they need. Besides, most of what we give them is stolen or given to the army. The people who need it most get very little, if anything.

9. Ship the U.N. Headquarters to an isolated island someplace. We don't need the spies and fair weather friends here. Besides, the building would make a good homeless shelter or lockup for illegal aliens.

10. All Americans must go to charm and beauty school. That way, no one can call us 'Ugly Americans' any longer. The language we speak is ENGLISH. They learn it…or LEAVE…Now, isn't that a winner of a plan?

'The Statue of Liberty is no longer saying, 'Give me your tired, your poor, your huddled masses.' She's got a baseball bat and she's yelling, 'You want a piece of me?'

273

I OWE MY MOTHER

My mother taught me **To Appreciate a Job Well Done**: "if you're going to kill each other, do it outside. I just finished cleaning."

My mother taught me **Religion**: "You better pray that will come out of the carpet."

My mother taught me about **Time Travel**: "If you don't straighten up, I'm going to knock you into the middle of next week."

My mother taught me **Logic**: "Because I said so, that's why."

My mother taught me **More Logic**: "If you fall out of that swing and break your neck, you're not going to the store with me."

My mother taught me **Foresight:** "Make sure you wear clean underwear, in case you're in an accident."

My mother taught me **Irony**: "Keep crying, and I'll give you something to cry about."

My mother taught me about the science of **Osmosis**: "Shut your mouth and eat your supper."

My mother taught me about **Contortionism**: "Will you look at that dirt on the back of your neck."

My mother taught me about **Stamina**: "You'll sit there until all that spinach is gone."

My mother taught me about the **Weather:** "This room of yours looks as if a tornado went through it."

My mother taught me about **Hypocrisy:** "If I told you once, I've told you a million times. Don't exaggerate!"

My mother taught me the **Circle of Life:** "I brought you into this world, and I can take you out."

My mother taught me about **Behavior Modification:** "Stop acting like your father!"

My mother taught me about **Envy:** "There are millions of less fortunate children in this world who don't have wonderful parents like you do."

My mother taught me about **Anticipation:** "Just wait until we get home."

My mother taught me about **Receiving:** "You are going to get it when you get home!"

My mother taught me **Medical Science:** "If you don't stop crossing your eyes, they are going to get stuck that way."

My mother taught me **ESP:** "Put your sweater on; don't you think I know when you are cold?"

My mother taught me **Humor:** "When that lawn mower cuts off your toes, don't come running to me."

My mother taught me **How to Become an Adult:** "If you don't eat your vegetables, you'll never grow up."

My mother taught me **Genetics:** "You're just like your father."

My mother taught me about my **Roots:** "Shut that door behind you. Do you think you were born in a barn?"

My mother taught me **Wisdom**: "When you get to be my age, you'll understand."

My mother taught me about **Justice**: "One day you'll have kids, and I hope they turn out just like you."

YOU GOT MALE

A little boy goes to his father and asks "Daddy, how was I born?" The father answers: "Well son, I guess one day you will need to find out anyway!

"Your mom and I first got together in a chat room on Yahoo. Then I set up a date via e-mail with your mom and we met at a cyber-café. We sneaked into a secluded room, where your mother agreed to a download from my hard drive. As soon as I was ready to upload, we discovered that neither one of us had used a firewall, and since it was too late to hit the delete button, nine months later a little Pop-Up appeared that said: 'You got Male!'"

OH, THE ANTICIPATION!

The Smiths were unable to conceive children and decided to use a surrogate father to start their family. On the day the proxy father was to arrive, Mr. Smith kissed his wife goodbye and said, "Well, I'm off now. The man should be here soon."

Half an hour later, just by chance, a door-to-door baby photographer happened to ring the doorbell, hoping to make a sale. "Good morning, Ma'am, he said, "I've come to...."

"Oh, no need to explain," Mrs. Smith cut in, embarrassed, "I've been expecting you."

"Have you really?" said the photographer. "Well, that's good. Did you know babies are my specialty?"

"Well that's what my husband and I had hoped. Please come in and have a seat." After a moment she asked, blushing, "Well, where do we start?"

"Leave everything to me. I usually try two in the bathtub, one on the couch, and perhaps a couple on the bed. And sometimes the living room floor is fun. You can really spread out there."

"Bathtub, living room floor? No wonder it didn't work out for Harry and me!"

"Well, Ma'am, none of us can guarantee a good one every time. But if we try several different positions and I shoot from six or seven angles, I'm sure you'll be pleased with the results."

"My, that's a lot!" gasped Mrs. Smith.

"Ma'am, in my line of work a man has to take his time. I'd love to be in and out in five minutes, but I'm sure you'd be disappointed with that."

"Don't I know it," said Mrs. Smith quietly.

The photographer opened his briefcase and pulled out a portfolio of his baby pictures. "This was done on the top of a bus," he said.

"Oh, my God!" Mrs. Smith exclaimed, gasping at her throat.

"And these twins turned out exceptionally well – when you consider their mother was so difficult to work with."

"She was difficult?" asked Mrs. Smith.

"Yes, I'm afraid so. I finally had to take her to the park to get the job done right. People were crowding around four and five deep to get a good look."

"Four and five deep?" said Mrs. Smith, her eyes wide with amazement.

"Yes," the photographer replied. "And for more than three hours, too. The mother was constantly squealing and yelling – I could hardly concentrate, and when darkness approached I had to rush my shots. Finally, when the squirrels began nibbling on my equipment, I just had to pack it all in."

Mrs. Smith leaned forward. "Do you mean they actually chewed on your, up…equipment?"

"It's true, Ma'am, yes. Well, if you're ready, I'll set-up my tripod and we can get to work right away."

"Tripod?"

"Oh yes, Ma'am. I need to use a tripod to rest my Canon on. It's much too big to be held in the hand very long."

Mrs. Smith fainted.

THE HUSBAND STORE

A brand new store has just opened in New York City that sells Husbands. When women go to choose a husband, they have to follow the instructions at the entrance:

"You may visit this store ONLY ONCE!" There are 6 floors and the value of the products increase as you ascend the flights. You may choose any item from a particular floor, or may choose to go up to the next floor, but you CANNOT go back down except to exit the building!

So, a woman goes to the Husband Store to find a husband.

On the 1st floor the sign on the door reads: Floor 1 – These men have jobs.

The 2nd floor sign reads: Floor 2 – These men Have Jobs and Love Kids.

The 3rd floor sign reads: Floor 3 - These men Have Jobs, Love Kids and are extremely good looking.

"Wow," she thinks, but feels compelled to keep going, so off to the 4th floor, and the sign reads: Floor 4 – These man Have Jobs, Love Kids, are Drop-dead Good Looking and Help with Housework.

"Oh, mercy me!" she exclaims, "I can hardly stand it!"

Still, she goes to the 5th floor and sign reads: Floor 5 – These men Have Jobs, Love Kids, are Drop-dead Gorgeous, help with

Housework, Have a Strong Romantic Streak and are Hung like a Shetland Pony.

She is so tempted to stay, but she goes to the 6th floor and the sign reads: Floor 6 – You are visitor 31,456,012 to this floor. There are no men on this floor. This floor exists solely as proof that women are impossible to please. Thank You for shopping at the Husband Store.

To avoid gender bias charges, the store's owner opens a New Wives store just across the street.

The 1st floor wives that love sex.

The 2nd floor has wives that love sex and have money.

The 3rd through 6th floors have NEVER BEEN VISITED.

VERY INTERESTING STUFF

In the 1400's a law as set forth in England that a man was allowed to beat his wife with a stick no thicker than his thumb. Hence we have "the rule of thumb."

Many years age in Scotland, a new game was invented. It was ruled "Gentlemen Only...Ladies Forbidden"...and thus the word GOLF entered into the English language.

The first couple to be shown in bed together on prime time TV were Fred and Wilma Flintstone.

Every day more money is printed for Monopoly than the U.S. Treasury.

Men can read smaller print than women can; women can hear better.

Coca-Cola was originally green.

It is impossible to lick your elbow.

The State with the highest percentage of people who walk to work: Alaska.

The percentage of Africa that is wilderness: 28% (now get this...). The percentage of North America that is wilderness: 38%.

The cost of raising a medium-size dog to the age of eleven: $16,400.

The average number of people airborne over the U.S. in any given hour: 61,000.

Intelligent people have more zinc and copper in their hair.

The first novel ever written on a typewriter: Tom Sawyer.

The San Francisco Cable cars are the only mobile National Monuments.

Each king in a deck of playing cards represents a great king from history:

    Spades – King David
    Hearts – Charlemagne
    Clubs – Alexander, the Great
    Diamonds – Julius Caesar

$111,111,111 \times 111,111,111 = 12,345,678,987,654,321$

If a statue in the park of a person on a horse has both front legs in the air, the person died in battle. If the horse has one front leg in the air the person died as a result of wounds received in battle. If the horse has all four legs on the ground, the person died of natural causes.

Only two people signed the Declaration of Independence on July 4th, John Hancock and Charles Thomson. Most of the rest signed on August 2, but the last signature wasn't added until 5 years later.

Question: Half of all Americans live within 50 miles of what? Answer: Their birthplace.

Question: Most boat owners name their boats? What is the most popular boat name requested? Answer: Obsession.

Question: If you were to spell out numbers, how far would you have to go until you would find the letter "A"? Answer: One thousand.

Question: What do bulletproof vests, fire escapes, windshield wipers, and laser printers all have in common? Answer: All were invented by women.

Question: Which day are there more collect calls than any other day of the year? Answer: Father's Day.

In Shakespeare's time, mattresses were secured on bed frames by ropes. When you pulled on the ropes the mattress tightened, making the bed firmer to sleep on. Hence the phrase…"goodnight, sleep tight."

It was the accepted practice in Babylon 4,000 years ago that for a month after the wedding, the bride's father would supply his son-in-law with all the mead he could drink. Mead is a honey beer and because their calendar was lunar based, this period was called the honey month, which we know today as the honeymoon.

In English pubs, ale is ordered by pints and quarts.… So in old England, when customers got unruly, the bartender would yell at them, "Mind your pints and quarts, and settle down." It's where we get the phrase "mind your P's and Q's."

Many years ago in England, pub frequenters had a whistle baked into the rim, or handle, of their ceramic cups. When they needed a refill, they used the whistle to get some service. "Wet your whistle" is the phrase inspired by this practice.

At least 75% of people who read this will try to lick their elbow!

LIVING IN 2008

You know you are living in 2008 when....

1. You accidentally enter your PIN on the microwave.
2. You haven't played solitaire with real cards in years.
3. You have a list of 15 phone numbers to reach your family of three.
4. You e-mail the person who works at the desk next to you.
5. Your reason for not staying in touch with friends and family is that they don't have e-mail addresses.
6. You pull up in your own driveway and use your cell phone to see if anyone is home to help you carry in the groceries.
7. Every commercial on television has a web site at the bottom of the screen.
8. Leaving the house without your cell phone, which you didn't even have the first 20 or 30 or 60) years of your life, is now a cause for panic and you turn around to go and get it.
9. You get up in the morning and go on line before getting your coffee.
10. You start tilting your head sideways to smile. :)
11. You're reading this and nodding and laughing.

THE 6 BEST SMART-ASS ANSWERS

Smart Ass Answer #6 - It was mealtime during a flight on American Airlines. "Would you like dinner?" the flight attendant asked John, seated in front. "What are my choices?" John asked. "Yes or No," she replied.

Smart Ass Answer #5 - A flight attendant was stationed at the departure gate to check tickets. As a man approached, she extended her hand for the ticket and he opened his trench coat and flashed her. Without missing a beat, she said, "Sir, I need to see your ticket not your stub."

Smart Ass Answer #4 - A lady was picking through the frozen turkeys at the grocery store but she couldn't find one big enough for her family. He asked a stock boy, "Do these turkeys get any bigger?" The stock boy replied, "No ma'am, they're dead."

Smart Ass Answer #3 - The cop got out of his car and the guy who was stopped for speeding rolled down his window. "I've been waiting for you all day," the cop said. The kid replied, "Yeah, well I got here as fast as I could." When the cop finally stopped laughing, he sent the kid on his way without a ticket.

Smart Ass Answer #2 - A truck driver was driving along on the freeway. A sign comes up that reads, "Low Bridge Ahead." Before he knows it, the bridge is right ahead of him and he gets stuck under the bridge. Cars are backed up for miles. Finally, a police car comes up. The cop gets out of his car and walks to the truck driver, puts his hands on his hips and says, "Got stuck, huh?" The truck driver says, "No, I was delivering this bridge and ran out of gas."

Smart Ass Answer of the Year - A college teacher reminds her class of tomorrow's final exam. "Now class, I won't tolerate any excuses for you not being here tomorrow. I might consider a nuclear attack or a serious personal injury, illness, or a death in you immediate family, but that's it, no excuses whatsoever!" A smart-ass guy in the back of the room raised his hand and asked, "What would you say if tomorrow I said I was suffering from complete and utter sexual exhaustion?" The entire class is reduced to laughter and snickering. When silence is restored, the teacher smiles knowingly at the student, shakes her head and sweetly says, "Well, I guess you'd have to write the exam with your other hand."

SERENITY

- Just before the funeral services, the undertaker came up to the very elderly widow and asked, "How old was your husband?" "98," she replied. "Two years older than me." "So you're 96," the undertaker commanded. She responded, "Hardly worth going home, isn't it?"

- Reporters interviewing a 104-year-old woman: "And what do you think is the best thing about being 104?" the reporter asked. She simply replied, "No peer pressure."

- The nice thing about being senile is you can hide your own Easter eggs.

- I've sure gotten old! I've had two bypass surgeries, a hip replacement, new knees, fought incontinence and diabetes, I'm half blind, can't hear anything quieter than a jet engine, take 40 different medications that make me dizzy, winded, and subject to blackouts. Have bouts with dementia. Have poor circulation; hardly feel my hands and feet anymore. Can't remember if I'm 85 or 92. Have lost all my friends. But, thank the Lord, I still have my driver's license.

- I feel like my body has gotten totally out of shape, so I got my doctor's permission to join a fitness club and start exercising. I decided to take an aerobics class for seniors. I bent, twisted, gyrated, jumped up and down, and perspired for an hour. But, by the time I got my leotards on, the class was over.

- An elderly woman decided to prepare her will and told her preacher she had two final requests. First, she wanted to be cremated, and second, she wanted her ashes scattered over Wal-Mart. "Wal-Mart?" the preacher exclaimed. "Why Wal-

Mart?" "Then, I'll be sure my daughter visits me twice a week."

- My memory's not as sharp as it used to be. Also, my memory's not as sharp as it used to be. Know how to prevent sagging? Just eat till the wrinkles fill out.

- It's scary when you start making the same noises as your coffee maker.

- These days about half the stuff in my shopping cart says, "for fast relief."

"HELLO FRIEND"

"They're standing on the corner and they can't speak English. I can't even talk the way these people talk.

"Why you ain't,
"Where you is,
"What he drive,
"Where he stay,
"Where he work,
"Who you be…

"And I blamed the kid until I heard the mother talk. And then I heard the father talk.

"Everybody knows it's important to speak English except these knuckleheads. You can't be a doctor with that kind of crap coming out of your mouth.

"In fact you will never get any kind of job making a decent living. People marched and were hit in the face with rocks to get an education and now we've got these knuckleheads walking around.

"The lower economic people are not holding up their end of this deal. These people are not parenting. They are buying things for kids - $200 sneakers for what?

"And they won't spend $200 for Hooked on Phonics. I am talking about these people who cry when their son is standing there in an orange suit.

"Where were you when he was 2? Where were you when he was 12? Where were you when he was 18 and how come you didn't know that he had a pistol? And where is the father? Or who is his father?

"People putting their clothes on backward: Isn't that a sign of something gone wrong? People with their hats on backward, pants down around the crack, isn't that a sign of something? Or are you waiting for Jesus to pull his pants up?

"Isn't it a sign of something when she has her dress all the way up and got all type of needles (piercing) going through her body? What part of Africa did this come from? We are not Africans. Those people are not Africans; they don't know a thing about Africa.

"With names like Shaniqua, Taliqua, and Mohammed and all of that crap, and all of them are in jail.

"Brown or black verses the Board of Education is no longer the white person's problem. We have got to take the neighborhood back.

"People use to be ashamed. Today a woman has eight children with eight different 'husbands' – or men or whatever you call them now.

"We have millionaire football players who cannot read. We have million-dollar basketball players who can't write two paragraphs. We, as black folks have to do a better job. Someone working at Wal-Mart with seven kids, you are hurting us.

"We have to start holding each other to a higher standard. We cannot blame the white people any longer. It's NOT about color…It's about behavior"

Bill Cosby

SMOKE SIGNALS

At her father's wake, a woman told her priest that ever since she was a child she and her father had discussed life after death. They had agreed that whoever went first would contact the other. They had discussed this again just two weeks before his death.

He died in her home and a few days after his death the smoke alarm in her garage went off. She had lived there for 28 years and it had never gone off before. She couldn't turn it off so she called the security company that installed it.

The next morning the smoke alarm sounded again...and the reason finally downed on her...she said aloud, "OK dad, I missed the signal yesterday, but I get it now! Thanks for letting me know that you are safe on the other side. Now turn the thing off so I don't have to call the security company again." And it went off.

She immediately called her priest to tell him the good news. His response: "Dear lady, if every time your father sends you a message, he sets off the smoke alarm, just where do you think he's calling from?"

THE DRUGGIST

Upon arriving home, a husband was met at the door by his sobbing wife. Tearfully she explained, "It's the druggist. He insulted me terribly this morning on the phone. I had to call multiple times before he would even answer the phone."

Immediately, the husband drove downtown to confront the druggist and demand an apology. Before he could say more than a word or two, the druggist told him, "Now, just a minute, listen to my side of it. This morning the alarm failed to go off, so I was late getting up. I went without breakfast and hurried out to the car, just to realize that I had locked the house with both house and car keys inside and had to break a window to get my keys.

"Then, driving a little too fast, I got a speeding ticket. Later, when I was about three blocks from the store, I had a flat tire. When I finally got to the store a bunch of people were waiting for me to open up. I got the store opened and started waiting on these people, and all the time the darn phone was ringing off the hook.

"Then I had to break a roll of nickels against the cash register drawer to make change, and they spilled all over the floor. I had to get down on my hands and knees to pick up the nickels and the phone was still ringing.

"When I came up I cracked my head on the open cash drawer, which made me stagger back against a showcase with a bunch of perfume bottles on it. Half of them hit the floor and broke. Meanwhile, the phone is still ringing with no let up, and I finally got back to answer it. It was your wife.

"She wanted to know how to use a rectal thermometer.

"And believe me, mister, as God is my witness, all I did was tell her."

APPLICATION FOR PERMISSION
TO DATE MY DAUGHTER

Note: this application will be incomplete and rejected unless accompanied by a complete financial statement, job history, lineage, and current medical report from your doctor.

NAME _____ DATE OF BIRTH _____

HEIGHT _____ WEIGHT _____ IQ _____ GPA _____

SOCIAL SECURITY # _____
DRIVER'S LICENSE # _____

BOY SCOUT RANK AND BADGES

_____

HOME ADDRESS _____
CITY/STATE _____ ZIP _____

Do you have parents? ____ Yes ____ No

Is one male and the other female? ____ Yes ____ No

If No, explain:

_____

ACCESSORIES SECTION:

    A. Do you own or have access to a van? ____ Yes ____ No

    B. A truck with oversized tires? ____ Yes ____ No

    C. A waterbed? ____ Yes ____ No

    D. A pickup with a mattress in the back? ____ Yes ____ No

E. A tattoo? _____ Yes _____ No

F. Do you have an earring, nose ring, pierced, tongue, pierced cheek or a belly button ring? _____ Yes _____No

(If you answered 'yes' to any of the above, discontinue application and leave premises immediately – I suggest running.)

ESSAY SECTION:
In 50 words or less, what does 'LATE' mean to you?

In 50 words or less, what does 'Don't Touch My Daughter' mean to you?

In 50 words or less, what does 'Abstinence' mean to you?

REFERENCES SECTION:

Church you attend: _____

How often do you attend _____

When would be the best time to interview your:
    Father? _____
    Mother? _____
    Pastor? _____

SHORT-ANSWER SECTION:
Answer by filling in the blank. Please answer freely, all answers are confidential.

    A. If I were shot, the last place I would want to be shot would be:

B. If I were beaten, the last bone I would want broken is my;

C. A woman's place is in the:

D. The one thing I hope this application does not ask me about is:

E. What do you want to do IF you grow up?

F. When I meet a girl, the thing I always notice about her first is:

I SWEAR THAT ALL INFORMATION SUPPLIED ABOVE IS TRUE AND CORRECT TO THE BEST OF MY KNOWLEDGE UNDER PENALTY OF DEATH, DISMEMBERMENT, NATIVE AMERICAN ANT TORTURE, CRUCIFIXION, ELECTROCUTION, CHINESE WATER TORTURE, RED HOT POKERS, AND HILLARY CLINTON KISS TORTURE.

Thank you for your interest, and it had better be genuine and non-sexual. Please allow four to six years for processing.

You will be contacted in writing if you are approved. Please do not try to call or write (since you probably can't, and it would cause you injury). If your application is rejected, you will be notified by two gentlemen wearing white ties carrying violin cases. (You might watch your back.)

NOTICE

Due to the present Economic Uncertainties, the light at the end of the tunnel will be turned off until further notice.

Compiler's Bio

Robert D. Kramer is a graduate of Ohio University and served in the US Air Force during the Vietnam era. He has worked in the corporate America banking for forty-two years. Robert is also Director Emeritus for the Salvador Dali Museum in St. Petersburg, Florida and past Director of the Mahaffee Theater, also located in St. Petersburg, FL.